THE COMPLETE BOOK OF MOVIE LISTS

"You spend all your life trying to do something they put people in asylums for."
Jane Fonda

THE COMPLETE BOOK OF MOVIE LISTS

by
NICHOLAS VAN DAALEN

Pagurian Press

DUTTON

Copyright© 1979 PAGURIAN PRESS LIMITED
Suite 1106, 335 Bay Street, Toronto, Canada

Photographs courtesy of The Ontario Film Institute

ISBN 0-525-06985-2
ISBN 0-525-03095-6

Printed and bound in Canada

CONTENTS

7009332

Introduction   7

1. Private Lives   9
2. The Stars   57
3. The Directors   115
4. The Studios   123
5. Controversial Topics   137
6. Silent Movies   149
7. Monsters and Westerns   161
8. Musicals   169
9. Trivia   177
10. Flesh and Fantasy   201
11. Nostalgia   217
12. Humor   231
13. Awards   241
14. The Best and the Worst   259
15. Numbers   275
16. Firsts and Lasts   281

Jon Voight is a misfit in the power-seeking, materialistic Hollywood of the seventies. He won an Oscar for Coming Home *(1979).*

INTRODUCTION

It has always been an ambition of mine to write a book about Hollywood and to call it *Inside Hollywood*. Or perhaps it should be called *Builders of the American Dream*. However, Kenneth Anger has already written about the first subject under a different title; and Stewart Holbrook a book about the latter subject that dealt mainly with the great American money makers.

This is a different book, and a book with a difference. It is the inside story from the *other* side. Lights, cameras, action. Make it alive! This is *their* story.

And why, after 60-plus years are we still fascinated by Hollywood and the Hollywood myth? Why is it that we want to believe in that never-never land where the beautiful, rich, and successful live lives as complex as their movie plots? And why are we so eager to find out the truth about these people who feed our fantasies?

Hollywood has always provided an escape route for our dreams, and this book is a journey along that yellow-brick road—paved with opinions, stories, facts, and more facts about and by the inside people. I have tried to satisfy our fantasies and curiosity with a whole host of quotes and lists by and about the stars, the directors, the producers, the misfits, the clowns, and everyone else that exists in and around the cauldron that was and is Hollywood. It is a highly opinionated book, and I have intended it to be so. But for anyone like me who has ever spent a blissful Saturday night with a bag of popcorn and a Hollywood movie I don't think you can help but be intrigued and amazed. I still am.

Nicholas Van Daalen
Hollywood, 1979

"To put it bluntly, I seem to be a whole superstructure with no foundation. But I'm working on the foundation."
Marilyn Monroe

1
PRIVATE LIVES

10 REVEALING QUOTATIONS MADE BY THE STARS ABOUT THEMSELVES

1. "I want to be alone."
   Greta Garbo

2. "I don't trust any bastard who doesn't drink."
   Humphrey Bogart

3. "I am by way of being a student of history. I know the Jester always pays, for the king inevitably kicks him downstairs."
   Charlie Chaplin

4. "I was a fourteen-year-old boy for thirty years."
   Mickey Rooney

5. "Well, I've played everything but a harp."
   Lionel Barrymore

6. "To put it bluntly, I seem to be a whole superstructure with no foundation. But I'm working on the foundation."
   Marilyn Monroe

7. "I've done everything I ever wanted to do. I've played Hamlet; I've had every woman I ever wanted. I have a son to carry on my name. I'm bored and I'm tired."
   John Barrymore, at fifty, before he started drinking himself to death—which took him ten years

8. "The most important thing a woman can have next to her talent, is her hairdresser."
   Joan Crawford

9. "Don't say yes until I've finished talking."
   Daryl Zanuck to one of his yes-men

10. "I don't pretend to be an ordinary housewife."
    Elizabeth Taylor

"I don't pretend to be an ordinary housewife."
Elizabeth Taylor

10

8 ACTRESSES WHO WERE INVOLVED IN HOLLYWOOD SEX AND DRUG SCANDALS

1. OLIVE THOMAS—1920

Hollywood's first major scandal. The former Ziegfeld showgirl and star of *The Flapper,* was found naked and dead, clothed only in a sable coat, a bottle of mercury granules still in her hand. The place: The Hotel Crillon in Paris. Married to Jack Pickford, Mary Pickford's brother, investigators later revealed a lurid private life with the cause of death probably suicide as a result of failing to purchase a supply of heroin for her husband Jack, a hopeless drug addict.

2. ALMA RUBENS—1929

One of Hollywood's best-known and best-loved dramatic actresses and the star of *Showboat* and *The Holy Bread,* revealed herself to be a chronic morphine addict, after being arrested on Hollywood Boulevard in January 1929. Pursued by two men, Miss Rubens began tearing off her clothes and, in the ensuing struggle with her two followers, stabbed one of them critically. The other gentleman, her doctor, then committed her to a local sanitarium where, again in a violent outburst, she stabbed her private nurse.

Following her eventual release after six months from a California state hospital for the insane, Miss Rubens tried to resume her career in New York without success. Returning to Hollywood she was arrested again, charged with possession of morphine. She was committed to hospital again, where, on January 22, 1933, she died, aged 33.

3. LITA GRAY—1927

Former child bit-player in two of Charlie Chaplin's films, Lita Gray became in 1924 one of the stars in his best-known movie *The Gold Rush*. Sixteen years old and pregnant, the ambitious teenager forced a shotgun marriage with Chaplin on November 24, 1924. It was the scandal of the year. Miss Gray's film footage of *The Gold Rush* was never used and Chaplin's child bride immediately retired from movie pictures. It was a profitable retirement. After two years and two sons, Miss Gray filed for divorce citing seduction, sexual perversity, gross immorality, as well as threatened murder and infidelity. On August 22, 1927, Miss Gray was awarded a $625,000 cash settlement out of court but not before the most intimate and lurid details of the doomed relationship had been dragged across the newspapers of North America.

4. MARION DAVIES—1924

The notorious relationship with the married William Randolph Hearst led to one of Hollywood's worst scandals on the yacht *Oneida* in 1924. The cruise, to celebrate producer-director Thomas H. Ince's forty-third birthday, also hosted fifteen other guests, among whom were actress Margaret Livingstone (Ince's mistress), Charlie Chaplin, Louella Parsons (a Hearst columnist), and twelve other movie friends and associates. Complete with jazz band, liquor, and champagne, the cruise had a tragic ending. Ince was to die of an acute "stomach disorder" after being taken from the yacht to Hearst's California mansion. However, this simple tragic tale concealed a far more sinister story. The jealous sixty-two-year-old Hearst, on the lookout for a rumored tryst between

Marion Davies was involved in one of the worst Hollywood sex scandals in 1924.

Clara Bow's telltale diary revealed a lurid love career in a famous 1930 court case. She entertained the entire University of Southern California football team!

the young Miss Davies and Mr. Chaplin, had evidently discovered the nude couple on one of the lower decks. The irate Hearst reached for his revolver, but with other guests arriving to Miss Davis's screams, it was Ince and not Chaplin who fell to the deck with a bullet in his head. Ince's body was cremated and the funeral held in Hollywood on November 21—six days after the cruise began. There was no official inquest, but persistent rumors caused the San Diego district attorney, Chester Kemply, to call for a further investigation. But the true story was never revealed, and the power of William Randolph Hearst and his press managed to quell the affair. There seemed to have been various pay-offs, but one guest in particular, Louella Parsons, secured for herself the coveted movie columnist role for the Hearst newspaper empire.

5. CLARA BOW—1930

After Clara Bow, the "It" girl, fired her trusted private secretary Daisy DeVoe, following an attempt at blackmail, Miss DeVoe sold the "inside" story of her boss's love career to the scandalous New York tabloid *Graphic*. There were instant headlines. Miss DeVoe had kept a detailed list of Miss Bow's amorous visitors including Eddie Cantor, Gary Cooper, Bella Lugosi, Rex Bell, and the entire University of Southern California football team—including John Wayne.

Miss Bow took her secretary to court where she was later convicted for theft and sent to jail, but when the infamous "It" girl's Paramount contract expired some months later, it was not renewed.

Clara Bow spent the greater part of the rest of her life suffering a series of nervous breakdowns in sanitariums.

6. MARY ASTOR—1935

One of the screen's great character actresses was also a detailed diary journalist and in one of Hollywood's most sensational divorce trials the contents of her slim, blue, leather-bound 1935 diary was filed as evidence by Miss Astor's physician-husband, Dr. Franklyn Thorpe. Although the request to admit the telltale diary was refused, the press somehow acquired the sordid details of several lasting jousts with the notorious playwright, George S. Kaufman—a man noted to have remarkable sexual prowess and staying power.

Both the court and the public were treated to a series of explicit sexual adventures, the faithful doctor won his divorce, and the popular Hollywood star returned (with daughter) to her mansion. Unscathed, a few years later she scored one of her greatest screen hits as the voluptuous villainess in *The Maltese Falcon.*

7. THELMA TODD—1935

One of Hollywood's most enigmatic murders remains unsolved today. The delightful and popular Thelma Todd, star of many Marx Brothers and Laurel and Hardy films, was found battered and bloody—slumped over the front seat of her white convertible on Monday, December 16, 1935. The ignition was on and her garage door was closed.

Despite her disfigured corpse, the jury declared a verdict of "death by carbon monoxide poisoning." But what was the true story? Miss Todd and her lover-director Roland West, co-managed the famous *Thelma Todd's Roadside Rest* —an extremely popular beach café. Subsequent questioning revealed that West and Miss Todd had had a bitter quarrel and the ensuing inquest also revealed that not only was the *Roadside Rest* losing money heavily, but that Miss Todd was also involved in a sordid affair with a San Francisco businessman. Later findings indicated an involvement with the notorious gangster Lucky Luciano who had threatened violence unless Miss Todd introduced a gambling casino into the upper floor of the café. The offer was turned down with the resulting tragic consequences.

Terrified of the powerful underworld, and despite powerful pleas by Miss Todd's lawyers, a second inquest was denied. It remains Hollywood's most mysterious finale.

8. LANA TURNER—1958

Recently separated from Lex Barker (Tarzan), Lana Turner at the height of her screen career became dangerously involved with Johnny Stompanato, the former bodyguard of gangster Mickey Cohen. Despite warnings and cruel publicity, MGM's movie queen gave up everything for the violent but well-endowed Italian. Hopelessly infatuated she became a slave to Stompanato—paying gambling debts and subjecting herself to brutal violence and threats.

Finally, during a scene at Miss Turner's mansion where Stompanato threatened the star with a stiletto, her daughter Cheryl Crane grabbed a nine-inch kitchen knife and plunged it into Stompanato, critically wounding him. It was a bloody scene, and expectedly it raised headlines across the United States. During the ensuing scandal the broken Lana Turner revealed further details of her lurid involvement—and the press had a field day. But, the verdict was unanimous—justifiable homicide.

Lana Turner weathered the bad publicity and, despite the new notoriety, star appearances in both *Peyton Place* and *Imitation of Life* made her one of Hollywood's wealthiest sirens.

8 ACTORS WHO WERE INVOLVED IN HOLLYWOOD SEX AND DRUG SCANDALS

1. ROSCOE "FATTY" ARBUCKLE—1921

Following a wild Labor Day party in San Francisco, the overweight comedian Roscoe Arbuckle, then under a three-million-dollar contract with Paramount, locked the young Chicago model and star, Virginia Rappé, in her bedroom and supposedly, in a drunken stupor, inserted a Coca-Cola bottle into her vagina, thus rupturing her bladder. She later died from peritonitis. The resulting three trials all ended in acquittal—mostly because of confused testimony. (Miss Rappé was later found not only to have a severe case of venereal disease, but also to be pregnant!) However, the public outcry ruined Arbuckle's career. Paramount cancelled his contract and the overweight actor became an alcoholic. He died penniless, a broken man, twelve years later.

2. WILLIAM DESMOND TAYLOR—1922

Nobody discovered who murdered William Taylor—a studio boss at Paramount. He was shot and his body discovered by his black manservant. Immediate investigations uncovered an incredible collection of ladies' lingerie and pornographic photographs; and that two well-known Hollywood actresses—Mabel Normand and Mary Miles Minter—had visited him during the night of his death. Mabel Normand was the last person to see him alive. The enigmatic murder of the handsome bachelor president of the Screen Directors Guild uncovered that Taylor was, in fact, William Deane-Tanner from New York, where he still had a wife and daughter. A renowned ladies' man, he had evidently been the cause of several Hollywood suicides, and had involvements in certain drug rings. Taylor's murder was never solved. But, it brought a scandalous end to both Miss Normand's and Miss Minter's screen careers.

3. WALLACE REID—1922

All Hollywood was shocked at the revelation that Wally Reid, one of the leading stars at Paramount Studios, was a chronic drug addict. Newspaper headlines resulted in his wife (Dorothy Davenport) committing him to a sanitarium to cure his morphine addiction. The incredibly popular movie star spent the rest of his brief life in hospital in a padded cell, where he eventually died, insane, on January 18, 1923.

4. ERICH VON STROHEIM—1923

When Irving Thalberg took over as production boss at MGM, the press and public were treated to an inside view of some of the most bizarre "production" activities ever held on location—anywhere. The German genius von Stroheim had directed such crowd-pleasers as *The Merry Widow, Merry-Go-Round,* and *The Wedding March,* as well as *Greed,* von Stroheim's lengthy study on avarice. But the stories behind the making of these movies would have made even better movies in themselves. They were orgies of such grandeur and scale that at times shooting continued without any stop for three whole days! The entire cast was involved and the imported extras were well paid not to reveal the inside and outside activities of the acting staff and film crew.

Always a lavish spender, von Stroheim—virtually blackballed by Thalberg and Louis B. Mayer—soon found it impossible to find backers. Out of work and penniless, one of the strangest geniuses Hollywood ever knew was forced to return to Europe.

6. ERROL FLYNN—1942

The charming, flamboyant, easy-going Tasmanian Errol Flynn had his Hollywood career rudely interrupted in 1942 when he was charged with one of California's most severe sexual crimes—statutory rape.

Two young girls, Peggy Satterlee and Betty Hansen, each under eighteen years old, claimed to have been seduced on separate occasions by the glamorous swashbuckler who had just completed *Captain Blood* and *The Adventures of Robin Hood* —two enormously successful Warner Brothers movies. Miss Satterlee was well known around the local Hollywood bars—and few realized she was under twenty—let alone eighteen. She was a well-experienced young lady. Miss Hansen's accusation was more humorous. She claimed to have been entertained to tennis, then a swim, and then to a bout of love-making by Flynn, where the actor had insisted on keeping his socks on! At the trial both girls had widely different

A bearded Errol Flynn, shown here with Valerie Hobson,
constantly shocked the outside world with his sexual exploits.

and diversified stories, and the jury took little more than a few minutes to clear and vindicate the actor. However, the District Attorney overruled the verdict and a second, lengthy trial ensued where Miss Satterlee and Miss Hansen went to town and described their wayward involvement with Flynn in lurid detail. The press had a field day, and although no one really believed the stories of the two supposedly injured girls, the handsome actor attained a notoriety that he had to live with for the rest of his acting career.

Eventually acquitted on all counts of rape, Errol Flynn resumed his career with little loss of popularity. The success of *Gentleman Jim,* the movie released shortly after the trial ended, proved to be the proof of the pudding. But a new phrase, "In like Flynn," was born; a phrase still used today, and still bringing back memories of an unfair but scandalous Hollywood joust with the law.

7. ROBERT MITCHUM—1948

Hollywood's most outspoken male star of the forties, and a legend in his own right today, was unceremoniously arrested for possession of marijuana during a midnight tryst at a starlet's Hollywood cottage on August 3, 1948. The starlet was blonde and attractive Lila Leeds.

It was an embarrasing arrest. Scheduled to address an enormous Los Angeles crowd the next day to celebrate the opening of National Youth Week, the guilty star had to not only cancel his practiced speech, but also to suffer the indignity of a two-month jail sentence.

On his release, and in danger of being blackballed by his own studio—controlled by David O. Selznick-Mitchum had his contract purchased by none other than Howard Hughes at RKO Studios. Retaining his popularity and unaffected by bad publicity, Robert Mitchum continued his laconic career and remains today one of the true giants of Hollywood.

8. ROMAN POLANSKI—1977

All Hollywood was aghast in 1977 when director Roman Polanski pleaded guilty in Santa Monica to having sex with a thirteen-year-old girl. He was immediately ordered to undergo a severe ninety-day psychiatric study at the California Men's Institute at Chino. Polanski, husband of the actress

*Roman Polanski was the central figure in one of Hollywood's
most sordid sex scandals involving a 13-year-old girl, but before
he could be brought to trial, the diminutive Polish director had
fled to Paris.*

Sharon Tate who had been brutally murdered a few years earlier, had admitted in an earlier court session that he had had "unlawful sexual intercourse" with the girl (whose name was not revealed because of her minor status) the previous March at the Beverley Hills home of actor Jack Nicholson. Nicholson was away at the time. Polanski had evidently taken her to the actor's mansion for a photosnapping session for *Vogue* magazine.

The dapper, 5'2" Polish director, who had just witnessed enormous success with *Rosemary's Baby* and *Chinatown*, was scheduled to direct the film *Hurricane* in Tahiti. But producer Dino de Laurentis dropped Polanski from the picture because of bad publicity and mounting costs caused by the delay while he was in prison.

Following his release from prison in January 1978, after forty-two days of psychiatric care, the director was ordered again to face trial where he stood to receive a sentence ranging up to fifty years in the State Penitentiary. Five previously scheduled other charges, including the use of drugs to permit rape, were dropped at the request of the girl's parents so that she might be spared the ordeal of the trial. But, before he could be brought to trial, the diminutive director fled the country and took up residence in Paris where he lives today. To date he has still not been brought to trial and has still not set foot in the United States.

10 MOVIE CAREERS THAT ENDED BADLY FOR HOLLYWOOD STARS

1. Veronica Lake, Alan Ladd's sultry partner, dissipated her looks with heavy drinking. Expelled from Hollywood, she was discovered a second time in 1962 working as a waitress and then again when she was arrested in New York for drunkenness. Her biography *Veronica* published in the late sixties again drew attention to the faded star, but she died in 1973 a broken person. Her four marriages had ended in divorce.

2. Betty Hutton—the blonde bombshell—was one of stardom's brighter stars in the early fifties. However, when her Para-

mount contract was not renewed, her impossible demands steered other studios away from her and her movie career was never resumed. She was last heard of working in New York for the Salvation Army.

3. Despite Oscars for best actress in *The Great Ziegfeld* (1936) and *The Good Earth* (1937) Luise Rainer's contract was never re-signed by the all-powerful mogul Louis B. Mayer at MGM. Out of work, the actress returned to her native Vienna.

4. When Louise Brooks at the top of her career walked out on her Paramount contract in 1929 she was not allowed a second chance. Returning to Hollywood in 1936 she was given only second-rate bit parts. Fame eluded her until over twenty years later when her European films were discovered.

5. In 1942 Peggy Ann Garner won a special award for *A Tree Grows in Brooklyn* She was an attractive highly paid child star with a rosy career ahead of her. But her movie career fizzled when she grew up to be a rather pasty-faced, plain, and unattractive young woman. MGM dropped her and she left the movie world for ever.

6. When Jean Peters married Howard Hughes, Hollywood lost one of its brightest and most attractive stars. She agreed never to make any more movies while married to the all-powerful millionaire recluse.

7. Carroll Baker was the girl most likely to succeed Marilyn Monroe but *The Carpetbaggers, Harlow,* and an ill-timed trashy version of *The Marilyn Monroe Story* left Paramount disillusioned. Her eventual downfall came when the giant Hollywood studio forced her to leave America for Rome where both her career and her marriage ended.

8. Dolores Hart could never stand the false realism of the celluloid screen. Wild parties and faded romances eventually led her to religion. Now a nun, Sister Dolores leads a life far away from Hollywood.

9. The star of *The Jolson Story,* Larry Parkes, was subjected to Hollywood's now infamous blacklisting during the McCarthy hearings in the forties. His movie career never recovered.

10. Sal Mineo, the boy starlet from *Rebel without a Cause,* never really lived up to his expectations. A flamboyant homosexual, he was brutally murdered in a parking lot, out of work and almost destitute.

10 TRUE TO LIFE SCREEN PORTRAYALS

1. Ruthlessly ambitious musical comedy star Joan Crawford played the part of a ruthlessly ambitious musical comedy star in *Torch Story.*

2. Plagued with domestic troubles, Lana Turner played a re-enactment of her own domestic woes in *Imitation of Life.*

3. Hollywood's infamous lover played the part of the world's greatest lover in *The Adventures of Don Juan* —Errol Flynn.

4. Tempestuous playgirl Ava Gardner played the part of an international playgirl in *The Sun Also Rises.*

5. Recently married Eddie Fisher and Debbie Reynolds played the lead roles in *Bundle of Joy* soon after Debbie Reynolds had given birth to baby Carrie Fisher.

6. Ambitious young starlet Linda Darnell played the part of an ambitious young girl being groomed for stardom in *Star Dust.*

7. Ex-alcoholic Bing Crosby played the part of a reformed alcoholic in *The Country Girl.*

8. Jack Lemmon, in the throes of a painful struggle with alcohol, starred in the film *Days of Wine and Roses* about a man with a similar problem.

9. William Randolph Hearst's mistress Marion Davies starred in the film *Blondie of the Follies* about a Ziegfeld showgirl who was kept by a wealthy tycoon.

10. Diane Keaton and Woody Allen, recently divorced, played mixed-up lovers trying in vain to make a go of a mixed-up situation in *Annie Hall.*

*Joan Crawford played a ruthlessly ambitious musical comedy
star in* Torch Song *(1953)—almost certainly Hollywood's most
true-to-life screen portrayal.*

Jack Lemmon, in the throes of a painful struggle with alcohol, starred in the film Days of Wine and Roses *about a man with a similar problem.*

Plagued by scandal and domestic troubles, Lana Turner often played similar roles in her movies.

10 HEADLINES THAT TERRORIZED THE STARS AND SHOCKED THE OUTSIDE WORLD

1. How mental sadist Ali Khan loused up Gene Tierney's psyche . . . he refused to marry her.

2. Errol Flynn and his two-way mirror . . . pheasant under glass wasn't the only dish served.

3. Why girls call Sonny Tufts, a cannibal . . . he ate his way right out of the movies.

4. Kim Novak and Sammy Davis, Jr . . . in Hollywood there's no such thing as a color line.

5. Frank Sinatra—Tarzan of the boudoir . . . the poor girl got practically no sleep for days.

6. Why Deanna Durbin won't come back . . . she sang her swan song in a lonely canyon, on a car seat.

7. Lana Turner and Ava Gardner . . . no males in sight but the girls had their hair down.

8. Why did Johnny Ray try to break down Paul Douglas's door? . . . The slim, handsome boy slipped out of Room 420 at the Dorchester Hotel in his birthday suit.

9. Lizabeth Scott is the call girls' call book . . . she took up with Paris's most notorious lesbian queen!

10. How Terry Moore became a Turkish delight . . . they all gasped when Terry sat down to pose.

Confidential Magazine

10 MYSTERIOUS HOLLYWOOD DEATHS AND RUMORS

1. Was Marilyn Monroe murdered by the CIA because she had inside information about President Kennedy's assassination? Or did she really die from an overdose of sleeping pills?

2. Was Bruce Lee the victim of the secret Kung Fu society or the

How did Montgomery Clift die? His emaciated body was found naked and drugged in a New York apartment—still wearing dark glasses.

Black Hand? Did he die of a brain injury? Or did he, in fact, die of an allergic drug reaction?

3. Did George Reeves (T.V.'s Superman) commit suicide? Or was his mangled gunshot body, the victim of a brutal murder, somehow connected to the filming of *From Here to Eternity*?

4. What was the cause of Rudolph Valentino's death? Did he die of peritonitis? Or was his death an intentional act on his part that put an end to a movie career that had reached its zenith, and a sordid love triangle that involved two of Hollywood's most notorious lesbians?

5. Is James Dean dead? Or is he really a vegetable kept alive by hospital machines in Milwaukee? Or did he commit suicide—a mixed-up teenage idol torn between love for Pier Angeli and his own homosexual leanings?

6. How did Montgomery Clift die? His emaciated body was found naked and drugged in his friend Lorenzo James's apartment in New York. He was still wearing dark glasses. Was it a case of accidental death or death because of severe malnutrition? Or did suicide bring a tragic life and career to its inevitable end?

7. When Carole Landis was found dead on her bathroom floor there was little doubt that an overdose of sleeping pills had put an end to her unhappy life. It was a clear case of suicide. But what triggered her critical act? Was the reason Rex Harrison? And is this the reason the debonair British actor returned to London and his wife Lilli Palmer—far from the U.S. press?

8. Did Mario Lanza die of a heart attack? Or did he in fact eat and drink his way out of his career and out of his life? The temperamental singing star had trouble keeping both jobs and weight down—drugs, booze, and obesity may have been the true cause of death.

9. A heart attack was the cause of death attributed to the turbulent Latin star Maria Montez in the fifties. But the former Universal headliner was found naked in an almost boiling saline bath in Europe, out of work and out of money.

10. Legal problems, weight problems, alcohol, and an almost nonexistent career plagued the blonde bombshell Jayne Mansfield during the last four months of her life. Was it really an accident that ended her downhill life on a dark Louisiana highway in 1967?

10 FIRST SEX EXPERIENCES

1. My girl friends were all telling me how much fun sex was (when I was fourteen)—as long as I didn't go all the way. So I just did it all at once with this guy next door ... a little Italian guy. When we'd finished I said "Is this it?" He said "Yeah." And I said, "Well you can go home."

   Cher

2. I lost my virginity and passed geometry all in the same summer. That was 1963. My sister said "Congratulations."

   Henry Winkler

3. I almost went all the way when I was thirteen. I was hanging out with an older crowd in Miami—guys who were seventeen/eighteen. They introduced me to a house of ill repute where I hired a forty-year-old woman. I was scared. All I remember is the mosquitoes bit my arse off. It wasn't a very romantic experience.

   James Caan

4. He was gorgeous. He looked like Jean-Paul Belmondo. We sang together in the Temple choir. We sat down on the sofa and started to kiss. I guess we were both eager. There wasn't any foreplay. None. We just walked in, sat down on this afghan ... and awkwardly went to it. I knew something was going on, but I didn't know what. I didn't feel a thing. I didn't even know when he left the house. Virgins bleed you know. After he left, I looked down and there was blood all over the afghan. I went hysterical. I rinsed the blood out of it under the cold water faucet.

   Dyan Cannon

5. When I was eight Thelma, who was an older woman of about nineteen, took me out into a tent in the back yard and taught me the facts of life—literally. If it was a shock, then it was a delightful shock. I like to think that I was her star pupil.

   Joseph Cotton

6. I lost my virginity when I was twenty-one. He was an older guy, older than me. I was working as a waitress. I told him I was a virgin ... and we went to his place. I was frightened. Emotionally, physically too, probably, because I didn't know what was coming. It was weird. Afterwards he felt like being close. He was saying warm things. "I can't believe you're a virgin." But my guilt was so great I was saying "Let me out of here."

   Sally Kellerman *The First Time*

7. At three in the morning I got up to use the bathroom. Suddenly Conrad (Nagel) rose from his armchair, threw back my bed covers, and before I could protest the dire deed was done. One might say I was surprised out of my virginity. I was twenty.

   Joan Fontaine *No Bed of Roses*

8. The first time I had an affair was in a parked car in a parking lot in Harvard Square. She was older—twenty-two or twenty-three. It wasn't my car—a Model A or something ... a convertible with the old stick gear shift. We're in the seat and I'm going crazy. Finally, I'm upside down and my feet go through a rip in the goddamned canvas and one of them gets caught. I'm moving around trying to get my foot out—she thinks I'm terrific. All of a sudden a voice and a flashlight say "Who is that? Who's in there?" I said "Someone's coming," and she said "Not yet." I'll never forget it.

   Jack Lemmon *The First Time*

9. Needless to say, I was a virgin when I married, like my mother before me, and her mother before her.

   Debbie Reynolds

10. I was thirteen, and he (my music teacher) must have been about twenty-one. I had been in this amateur show at the Royal Theatre and he had walked me there and back. It was winter and I had on my fur coat, and I was standing on the stairs, one step above him. I told him I had done it before. I wanted to see what it was like. He said "Are you sure you've done this before?" and I said "Sure, a couple of times." It hurt the first couple of times, but I wasn't frightened. After the first couple of times it felt good.

    Mae West

Mae West lost her virginity when she was thirteen!

10 GREAT HOLLYWOOD RUMORS

1. Mae West is a female impersonator.

2. Marlene Dietrich and Greta Garbo are gentlemen at heart.

3. Rudolph Valentino was the impotent plaything of two notorious lesbians: Nazimova and Natasha Rambova.

4. James Dean's sexual preferences won him the nickname "the human ashtray."

5. Charlie Chaplin's favorite song was "Thank Heaven for Little Girls."

6. Clark Gable and Loretta Young produced a child—adopted by Miss Young.

7. Both Joan Crawford and Marilyn Monroe starred in pornographic movies to help pay the rent.

8. Jean Harlow died trying to induce the abortion of a child fathered by William Powell.

9. Clara Bow hosted the entire U.C.L.A. football team in a single night or more.

10. Angie Dickinson was John F. Kennedy's favorite movie star.

7 STARS THAT HAD TO HAVE EXTRAORDINARY MAKE-UP BEFORE PRACTICALLY EVERY FILM

1. HAROLD LLOYD Having lost the thumb and index finger on his right hand he eventually resorted to wearing latex dummies. Off screen he also usually wore gloves.

2. BING CROSBY His lack of hair could easily be replaced by an expensive wig; but his large jutting ears had to be glued down with a special spirit gum. In later years, however, the famous crooner let his ears stick out quite normally—the world didn't care.

36

Bing Crosby's lack of hair could easily be replaced by an expensive wig, but his large, jutting ears had to be glued down with special spirit gum.

3. FRED ASTAIRE Almost completely bald, the miniature dancer always wore darker hair pieces and maintained his image both on and off screen.

4. PETER FALK Wears a glass eye.

5. MARGARET DUMONT Is completely bald and always had to wear a wig.

6. IDA LUPINO Also, almost completely bald. The famous Warner Brothers star always wore wigs.

7. CAROL CHANNING Constant bleaching has almost totally damaged the famous star's hair. She now *always* wears wigs.

10 STARS OTHER STARS HATED

1. Jeanette MacDonald and Greer Garson were the only two women Clark Gable ever disliked.

2. George Raft and Edward G. Robinson detested each other and with perverse delight.

3. Bud Abbott and Lou Costello's comedy partnership was not all peaches and cream. Costello was suing Abbott for $222,000 in unpaid royalties when he died in 1959.

4. The Bette Davis-Miriam Hopkins feuds and brawls during the making of *Old Acquaintance* lasted long after the filming stopped.

5. Ray Milland refused to play love scenes with an "old bag" like Marlene Dietrich during the filming of *Golden Earrings*. He still shows his contempt for the aging actress.

6. Vivien Leigh refused to continue to play love scenes in *Gone With the Wind* unless Clark Gable remedied the foul odor produced by his dentures.

7. Tyrone Power always said that Kim Novak confused bad manners with temperament. Their love scenes in *The Eddy Duchin Story* were faked.

Vivien Leigh refused to continue to play love scenes in Gone With the Wind *unless Clark Gable remedied the foul odor produced by his dentures.*

8. Ida Lupino was so irritated with Humphrey Bogart's sarcasm in *High Sierra* that she refused ever to be rehearsed with him again.

9. Joan Fontaine thought Cary Grant "an incredible boor." Their on-screen relationship in *Suspicion* was not what it seemed to be.

10. Errol Flynn was considered a good-looking nothing by Bette Davis during the filming of *The Private Lives of Elizabeth and Essex* (1939). A stage slap practically knocked Flynn out cold and their relationship remained hostile throughout their Hollywood careers.

Bette Davis waged several movie feuds. Those with Errol Flynn and Miriam Hopkins lasted long after filming stopped.

10 WELL-KNOWN ACTORS WHO HAVE HAD TO WEAR WIGS ON SCREEN

1. Frank Sinatra
2. Bing Crosby
3. Fred Astaire
4. Burt Reynolds
5. Gary Cooper

6. David Niven
7. Humphrey Bogart
8. Rex Harrison
9. Sean Connery
10. Henry Fonda

10 MORE ACTORS WHO HAVE TO WEAR WIGS

1. Laurence Olivier
2. Fred MacMurray
3. Peter Sellers
4. Robert Montgomery
5. James Stewart

6. George Burns
7. Charlton Heston
8. Ray Milland
9. Gene Kelly
10. John Wayne

7 ACTORS WHO HAVE HAD FACE LIFTS

1. Gary Cooper
2. Henry Fonda
3. Jean-Pierre Aumont
4. Dean Martin

5. Elvis Presley
6. Jackie Gleason
7. Frank Sinatra

A facelift was partly responsible for Merle Oberon's ageless beauty.

10 ACTRESSES WHO HAVE HAD FACE LIFTS

1. Rita Hayworth
2. Lucille Ball
3. Marlene Dietrich
4. Lana Turner
5. Joan Crawford

6. Mary Pickford
7. Barbara Stanwyck
8. Merle Oberon
9. Debbie Reynolds
10. Elizabeth Taylor

10 ON-LOCATION ROMANCES THE PUBLIC NEVER HEARD ABOUT

1. Greta Garbo and John Gilbert— *Love* (1927)

2. Clara Bow and Gary Cooper— *Children of Divorce* (1927)

3. Marlene Dietrich and Gary Cooper— *Morocco* (1930)

4. Loretta Young and Spencer Tracy— *Man's Castle* (1933)

5. Marion Davis and Dick Powell— *Hearts Divided* (1936)

6. Jack Benny and Ann Sheridan—*George Washington Slept Here* (1942)

*Gene Kelly (with Shirley MacLaine). The popular actor-danc-
er-director has always had to wear a wig for filming.*

7. Joan Crawford and Richard Egan—*The Damned Don't Cry* (1950)

8. Dorothy Dandridge and Otto Preminger—*Carmen Jones* (1954)

9. Marilyn Monroe and Yves Montand—*Let's Make Love* (1960)

10. Jane Fonda and Donald Sutherland— *Klute* (1971)

10 ON-LOCATION ROMANCES THE PUBLIC DID HEAR ABOUT

1. Clark Gable and Loretta Young—*The Call of the Wild* (1935)

2. Glenn Ford and Rita Hayworth—*The Loves of Carmen* (1948)

Cary Grant's love affair with Sophia Loren was given a great deal of attention in the actress's 1978 autobiography.

John Travolta and Lily Tomlin paired to create a well-publicized on-location romance in 1978.

3. Elizabeth Taylor and Montgomery Clift— *A Place in the Sun* (1951)

4. Spencer Tracy and Katharine Hepburn—*Pat and Mike* (1952)

5. Elvis Presley and Ann Margaret— *Love Me Tender* (1956)

6. Cary Grant and Sophia Loren— *Houseboat* (1958)

7. Elizabeth Taylor and Richard Burton— *Cleopatra* (1963)

8. Peter Bogdanovich and Cybill Shepherd— *The Last Picture Show* (1971)

9. Ali MacGraw and Steve McQueen— *The Getaway* (1972)

10. John Travolta and Lily Tomlin— *Moment by Moment* (1978)

Tyrone Power, probably the best looking leading man ever, had one problem—he had too much hair.

5 STARS WHO HAD TOO MUCH HAIR

1. Rita Hayworth
2. Barbara Stanwyck
3. Ginger Rogers

4. Robert Preston
5. Tyrone Power

3 ACTORS WHO HAD TO HAVE THEIR CHEST SHAVED FOR MOVIE MAKING

1. William Holden   2. Jeffrey Hunter   3. Jeff Chandler

10 VERY SHORT MOVIE ACTORS

1. Alan Ladd

2. Humphrey Bogart

3. Robert Redford

4. James Mason

5. Sammy Davis Jr.

6. Jack Nicholson

7. James Cagney

8. Bing Crosby

9. Charlie Chaplin

10. Fred Astaire

James Cagney won an Oscar for Yankee Doodle Dandy
(1942). He was one of Hollywood's shortest actors.

50

10 DIMINUTIVE MOVIE ACTRESSES

1. Elizabeth Taylor
2. Norma Shearer
3. Carole Lombard
4. Veronica Lake
5. Ann Blyth

6. Mary Pickford
7. June Haver
8. Judy Garland
9. Terry Moore
10. Gloria Swanson

Carole Lombard become one of the most glamorous stars of the glamorous thirties, even though she was very short and practically flat-chested.

'During this depression, when the spirit of the people is lower than at any other time, it is a splendid thing that for just fifteen cents, an American can go to a movie and look at the smiling face of a baby and forget his troubles."
   Franklin D. Roosevelt

2 MOVIE STARS WHO USED FALSE CURLS

1. Mary Pickford   2. Shirley Temple

10 LITTLE-KNOWN FACTS ABOUT MOVIE ACTRESSES

1. Joan Crawford's body and face were completely covered in freckles.

Brigitte Bardot—nicknamed "Sex Kitten."

2. Carole Lombard was almost flat chested.

3. Marilyn Monroe had a terrible weight problem.

4. Marlene Dietrich achieved her classic sunken cheek/high cheekbone beauty by removing her upper rear molars.

5. Judy Garland not only had a chronic weight problem, but had to use a latex nose bridge to hide a pug nose.

6. Greta Garbo talks only about herself.

7. Although Audrey Hepburn claims she can eat tons of pasta and not gain weight, rumor has it that she diets constantly.

8. Bette Davis is a chain smoker.

9. Mary Pickford hated her "goody-goody" roles.

10. Jane Fonda has stand-ins do her nude scenes.

Judy Garland—a diminutive movie actress with a chronic weight problem.

10 FAMOUS HOLLYWOOD NICKNAMES

1. *America's Sweetheart*—Mary Pickford
2. *The Sex Kitten*—Brigitte Bardot
3. *The Duke*—John Wayne
4. *The King*—Clark Gable
5. *The Man of a Thousand Faces*—Lon Chaney
6. *The Clothes Horse*—Joan Crawford
7. *The Handsomest Man in the World*—Francis X. Bushman
8. *The Iron Butterfly*—Jeanette Macdonald
9. *The Great Profile*—John Barrymore
10. *The Platinum Blonde*—Jean Harlow

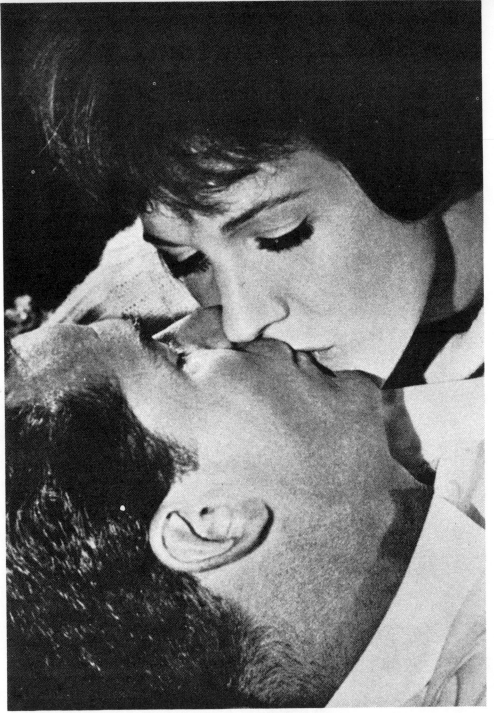

"Julie Andrews has that wonderful British strength that makes you wonder why they lost India."
Moss Hart

2
THE STARS

10 REVEALING STATEMENTS MADE BY THE STARS ABOUT EACH OTHER

1. BETTE DAVIS
"Surely no one but a mother could have loved Bette Davis at the height of her career."
Brian Aherne

2. KATHARINE HEPBURN
"She has a face that belongs to the sea and the wind, with large, rocking-horse nostrils and teeth that you just know bite an apple every day."
Cecil Beaton

3. GRETA GARBO
"What when drunk one sees in other women, one sees in Garbo sober."
Kenneth Tynan

4. MARLON BRANDO
"Marlon is now balding, paunchy. He remains an iconoclast without icons, a Messiah without a god. He is a genius without taste. He is a frightened lonely child."
Anna Kashfi, *Brando for Breakfast*

5. SPENCER TRACY
"I think Spencer always thought that acting was a rather silly way to make a living."
Katharine Hepburn

6. CHARLES CHAPLIN
"That obstinate, suspicious, egocentric, maddening, and lovable genius of a problem child."
Mary Pickford

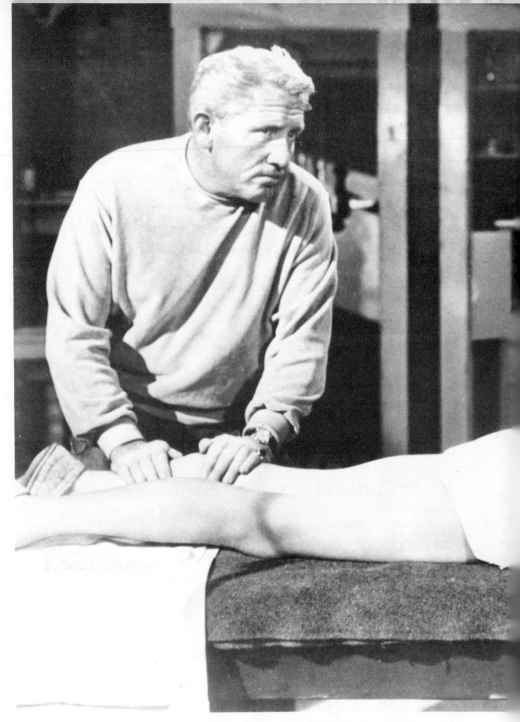

"*I think Spencer (Tracy) always thought that acting was a rather silly way to make a living.*"
Katharine Hepburn

7. JULIE ANDREWS

"She has that wonderful British strength that makes you wonder why they lost India."
Moss Hart

8. FRED ASTAIRE

"Can't act. Can't sing. Slightly bald. Can dance a little."
Studio talent scout, after Astaire's first screen test

9. SHIRLEY TEMPLE

"During this depression, when the spirit of the people is lower than at any other time, it is a splendid thing that for just fifteen cents, an American can go to a movie and look at the smiling face of a baby and forget his troubles."
Franklin D. Roosevelt

10. HARRY COHN

"You had to stand in line to hate him."
Hedda Hopper

THE 10 GREATEST STARS OF ALL TIME, BASED ON THE LENGTH OF THEIR FILM CAREERS

1. Charles Chaplin—54 years (1913-1967)

2. Mary Astor—48 years (1921-1969)

3. Bette Davis—47 years (1931-1978)

4. John Wayne—46 years (1930-1976)

5. Joan Crawford—45 years (1925-1970)

6. Edward G. Robinson—44 years (1929-1973)

7. Elizabeth Taylor—36 years (1942-1978)

8. Marlene Dietrich—34 years (1930-1964)

9. Cary Grant—33 years (1933-1966)

10. Clark Gable—30 years (1930-1960)

An early picture of Marlene Dietrich. Based on the length of her film career, she surely must be one of Hollywood's most lasting stars.

10 ACTRESSES WHO DIDN'T USE THEIR REAL NAMES

1. Constance Ockleman—Veronica Lake
2. Ruby Stevens—Barbara Stanwyck
3. Rosetta Jacobs—Piper Laurie
4. Shirley Schrift—Shelley Winters
5. Tula Ellice Finklea—Cyd Charisse
6. Lucille Langshanke—Mary Astor
7. Gladys Greene—Jean Arthur
8. Sara Jane Fulks—Jane Wyman
9. Frances Gumm—Judy Garland
10. Lily Chaudchoin—Claudette Colbert

10 ACTORS WHO DIDN'T USE THEIR REAL NAMES

1. Marion Morrison—John Wayne
2. James Stewart—Stewart Granger
3. Ernest Bickel—Frederic March
4. Isaiah Leopold—Ed Wynn
5. Bernard Schwartz—Tony Curtis
6. Guenther Schneider—Edward Arnold
7. Reginald Truscott-Jones—Ray Milland
8. William Henry-Pratt—Boris Karloff
9. Roy Scherer, Jr.—Rock Hudson
10. Emmanuel Goldenberg—Edward G. Robinson

8 ACTRESSES WHO PLAYED LEADS IN SILENT MOVIES AND WENT ON SUCCESSFULLY TO TALKIES

1. Janet Gaynor, *Seventh Heaven* (1927)
2. Mary Pickford, *Tess of the Storm Country* (1914)
3. Gloria Swanson, *Male and Female* (1919)
4. Lillian Gish, *The White Sister* (1923)
5. Dorothy Gish, *Hearts of the World* (1918)
6. Greta Garbo, *Flesh and the Devil* (1927)
7. Joan Crawford, *Our Dancing Daughters* (1928)
8. Za Su Pitts, *Greed* (1924)

8 ACTORS WHO PLAYED LEADS IN SILENT MOVIES AND WENT ON SUCCESSFULLY TO TALKIES

1. Douglas Fairbanks, *The Thief of Baghdad* (1924)
2. John Barrymore, *Beau Brummel* (1924)
3. Harold Lloyd, *Safety Last* (1923)
4. Buster Keaton, *Sherlock, Jr.* (1924)
5. Charles Chaplin, *The Circus* (1928)
6. Lon Chaney, *He Who Gets Slapped* (1924)
7. George Arliss, *The Man Who Played God* (1922)
8. Harry Langdon, *The Strong Man* (1926)

Doris Day turned down the part of Mrs. Robinson in The Graduate.

10 LEADS MOVIE STARS WERE OFFERED BUT TURNED DOWN AND DID NOT PLAY

1. Katharine Hepburn—Kitty Foyle in *Kitty Foyle* (1940)
2. Carole Lombard—Hildy Johnson in *His Girl Friday* (1940)
3. Bette Davis—Mildred Pierce in *Mildred Pierce* (1945)
4. Danny Thomas—Al Jolson in *The Jolson Story* (1946)
5. Mae West—Norma Desmond in *Sunset Boulevard* (1950)
6. Olivia de Havilland—Blanche du Bois in *A Streetcar Named Desire* (1951)
7. Georgie Jessel— *The Jazz Singer* (1953)
8. Montgomery Clift—in *On the Waterfront* (1954)
9. Doris Day—Mrs. Robinson in *The Graduate* (1967)
10. Tuesday Weld—Bonnie in *Bonnie and Clyde* (1967)

10 UNCHARACTERISTIC ROLES FOR 10 WELL-KNOWN STARS

1. In *Blonde Venus* (1932) Marlene Dietrich makes her entrance wearing only a gorilla skin and singing "Hot Voodoo."

2. Before his good-guy image was clearly defined, James Stewart turns out to be the murderer in *After the Thin Man* (1936).

3. Humphrey Bogart is a zombie vampire in *The Return of Dr. X* (1939).

4. Basil Rathbone livens up *The Adventures of Sherlock Holmes* (1939) by singing a music hall song.

5. An aging John Barrymore becomes a circus acrobat in his self-parodying role in *The Great Profile* (1940).

6. Betty Hutton has sextuplets in *The Miracle of Morgan's Creek* (1944), nine months after attending an all-night party.

7. Lon Chaney Jr. gets himself cured of being the wolf man and falls in love in *House of Dracula* (1945).

8. In *Summertime* (1955) Katharine Hepburn, a spinster vacationing in Venice, falls into a canal and in love with a married man (Rossano Brazzi).

9. In *Breakfast at Tiffany's* (1961) Mickey Rooney plays a daft Japanese—one of Audrey Hepburn's New York neighbors.

10. James Mason is ludicrous as a Chinese in the 1965 movie *Genghis Khan*.

6 STARS WHO PLAYED OTHER STARS' MOTHERS IN THE MOVIES

1. Greta Garbo played Scotty Beckett's mother in *Conquest* (1937).
2. Danielle Darrieux played Jane Powell's mother in *Rich, Young and Pretty* (1951).
3. Marjorie Main played Humphrey Bogart's mother in *Dead End* (1937).
4. Billie Burke played Joan Crawford's mother in *They All Kissed the Bride* (1942).
5. Sophie Tucker played Judy Garland's mother in *Broadway Melody* (1937).
6. Ruth Hussey played Jerry Lewis's mother in *That's My Boy* (1951).

6 STARS WHO PLAYED OTHER STARS' BROTHERS IN THE MOVIES

1. Jackie Cooper played Lana Turner's brother in *Ziegfeld Girl* (1941).
2. Dan Dailey played Margaret Sullavan's brother in *The Mortal Storm* (1940).
3. Mickey Rooney played Jean Harlow's brother in *Riffraff* (1935).
4. Claude Rains played Dick Powell's brother in *Hearts Divided* (1936).
5. Dean Martin played Wendy Hiller's brother in *Toys in the Attic* (1963).
6. Robert Wagner played Spencer Tracy's brother in *The Mountain* (1956).

10 HOLLYWOOD MISFITS

1. MARLON BRANDO

A mysterious mix of macho, magnetism, and myth, Marlon Brando is as much of an enigma in Hollywood today as he was almost thirty years ago when he played Stanley Kowalski in *A Streetcar Named Desire*. In real life he vacillates between a Hollywood mansion, a beloved South Sea island, and an Indian reservation. An advocate of civil rights reform in the fifties, more recently he has worked for American Indian civil rights.

2. ORSON WELLES

Orson Welles has never become a superstar. Although enormously gifted, in his youth he chose not to play romantic leads (which did not interest him) at a time (the 1940's) when the romantic image was a requisite for male stardom. Not content with being merely an actor, Orson Welles also wrote, directed, edited, produced, and even sound edited his movies.

His films have never been big box-office money makers and consequently, over the years, he has often not been able to raise enough money to bring his projects to completion.

3. JON VOIGHT

Not interested in the money, glamor, or publicity that go hand in hand with movie stardom, Jon Voight is preoccupied with perfecting his craft, ever self-doubting and skeptical of his talent. An idealist, he is a misfit in the power-seeking, materialistic Hollywood of the seventies.

4. ROBERT REDFORD

Although he has a reputation for being a political maverick and a misfit on the Hollywood social scene, Redford's films tend to emphasize not downplay his good looks—supposedly a source of embarassment to him—and even though his most popular films *(The Candidate, The Way We Were, All the President's Men)* have had a political slant, all have reflected the liberal and popular attitudes of the day—there is nothing controversial here.

5. JANE FONDA

Not long ago she was virtually blacklisted for her unpopular political views; today Jane Fonda is one of the most admired and respected actresses in North America. Recently

Robert Redford has a reputation for being a political maverick and a misfit on the Hollywood social scene.

Diane Keaton projects such vulnerability on the screen that audiences want to protect and look after her.

Over the last twenty-five years Paul Newman has acted in almost forty movies.

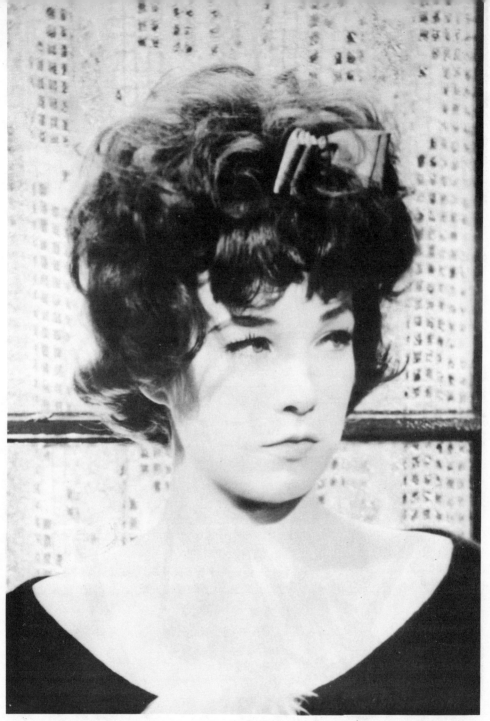

Shirley MacLaine has often been called a "kook" for being socially daring, rootless, and embracing unpopular political causes.

she won an Oscar for her performance in *Coming Home (1978),* in a role which brings together her personal views on the controversial Vietnam War and her considerable acting talent.

6. STEVE McQUEEN

Steve McQueen has been accused of being a publicity chaser, of being very difficult to work with, and of being exceedingly stubborn. No one, however, can deny the appeal of his on-screen personality—off-beat, aggressive, and sexy.

7. DIANE KEATON

Diane Keaton has almost made being neurotic attractive. Her screen persona is fragile and insecure; feeling inadequate she anticipates rejection. She projects such vulnerability that audiences want to protect and look after her.

8. PAUL NEWMAN

Over the last twenty-five years Paul Newman has acted in almost forty movies. Now one of the world's favorite movie stars and reputedly one of the best paid, he exudes an aura of respectability and success. But behind the publicity image lurks a lonely man, scarred by tragedy and a history of drinking and insecurity. He hates Hollywood and hates being a matinee idol, preferring character roles *(Hud, Butch Cassidy and the Sundance Kid, The Hustler, The Sting)* where he can really let himself go.

9. SHIRLEY MacLAINE

Called a "kook" because of her reputation for being socially daring, rootless, and embracing unpopular political causes, Shirley MacLaine in her movie roles has also shown many different faces—the hooker with a heart of gold, the straightforward sex object, the sick kook, and, most recently, the serious actress in *The Turning Point.*

10. PETER O'TOOLE

Peter O'Toole became an instant star after his performance in *Lawrence of Arabia* in 1962. Unfortunately he has never been able to rise to such heights again, despite many attempts at critical and box office success— *Becket,* 1964, *The Night of the Generals,* 1966, *The Lion in Winter,* 1966, and *The Ruling Class,* 1971. He projects too aristocratic an image for mass appeal.

Grace Kelly—one of 10 movie stars to have aged gracefully.

10 MOVIE STARS WHO HAVE AGED GRACEFULLY

1. Grace Kelly
2. Ingrid Bergman
3. Audrey Hepburn
4. Katharine Hepburn
5. Maggie Smith

6. Anne Bancroft
7. Greta Garbo
8. Julie Andrews
9. Dina Merrill
10. Lee Remick

10 MOVIE STARS WHO HAVE NOT AGED GRACEFULLY

1. Elizabeth Taylor
2. Mae West
3. Bette Davis
4. Brigitte Bardot
5. Barbra Streisand

6. Doris Day
7. Diana Dors
8. Rita Hayworth
9. Ava Gardner
10. Gloria Swanson

Neither Mae West nor the late Groucho Marx aged particularly gracefully. Both had controversially successful movie careers.

76

Diana Dors—another star who has not aged gracefully.

THE TOP 10 BOX OFFICE STARS OF THE
1930's—MALE AND FEMALE

1. Clark Gable
2. Shirley Temple
3. Joan Crawford
4. Will Rogers
5. Wallace Beery

6. Fred Astaire and Ginger Rogers
7. Norma Shearer
8. Marie Dressler
9. Janet Gaynor
10. Sonja Henie

Quigley Publications

THE TOP 10 BOX OFFICE STARS OF THE
1940's—MALE AND FEMALE

1. Bob Hope
2. Bing Crosby
3. Betty Grable
4. Humphrey Bogart
5. Clark Gable

6. Bud Abbott and Lou Costello
7. Gary Cooper
8. Spencer Tracy
9. Greer Garson
10. James Cagney

Quigley Publications

THE TOP 10 BOX OFFICE STARS OF THE
1950's—MALE AND FEMALE

1. John Wayne
2. James Stewart
3. Gary Cooper
4. Bing Crosby
5. Dean Martin and
   Jerry Lewis

6. Bob Hope
7. Frank Sinatra
8. William Holden
9. Randolph Scott
10. Marilyn Monroe

Quigley Publications

Clint Eastwood and William Holden today. Both remain top box-office stars.

Elvis Presley discarded his famous guitar in 1962 to star in Girls! Girls! Girls!

THE TOP 10 FEMALE BOX OFFICE STARS OF THE 1960's

1. Elizabeth Taylor
2. Doris Day
3. Julie Andrews
4. Sandra Dee
5. Barbra Streisand

6. Shirley MacLaine
7. Katharine Hepburn
8. Ann Margret
9. Debbie Reynolds
10. Katharine Ross

Quigley Publications

THE TOP 10 BOX OFFICE STARS OF THE 1960's—MALE AND FEMALE

1. John Wayne
2. Elizabeth Taylor
3. Doris Day
4. Paul Newman
5. Jack Lemmon

6. Elvis Presley
7. Rock Hudson
8. Julie Andrews
9. Richard Burton
10. Sandra Dee

Quigley Publications

THE TOP 10 MALE BOX OFFICE STARS OF THE 1960's

1. John Wayne
2. Paul Newman
3. Jack Lemmon
4. Elvis Presley
5. Rock Hudson

6. Richard Burton
7. Steve McQueen
8. Sean Connery
9. Jerry Lewis
10. Lee Marvin

Quigley Publications

THE TOP 10 BOX OFFICE STARS OF THE
1970's—MALE AND FEMALE

1. Clint Eastwood
2. Steve McQueen
3. Paul Newman
4. Barbra Streisand
5. John Wayne

6. Robert Redford
7. Charles Bronson
8. Burt Reynolds
9. Woody Allen
10. Al Pacino

Quigley Publications

THE TOP 10 FEMALE BOX OFFICE STARS OF THE
1970's

1. Barbra Streisand
2. Ali MacGraw
3. Tatum O'Neal
4. Faye Dunaway
5. Diane Keaton

6. Julie Christie
7. Jane Fonda
8. Goldie Hawn
9. Sissy Spacek
10. Liza Minnelli

Quigley Publications

THE TOP 10 MALE BOX OFFICE STARS OF THE
1970's

1. Clint Eastwood
2. Steve McQueen
3. Paul Newman
4. John Wayne
5. Robert Redford

6. Charles Bronson
7. Burt Reynolds
8. Woody Allen
9. Al Pacino
10. Dustin Hoffman

Quigley Publications

Steve McQueen is certainly one of Hollywood's top box office stars of the 1970's.

Barbra Streisand—one of the top ten female box office stars of the 1970's and a powerful figure in the Hollywood of today.

Lou Costello played some movie leads in drag.

10 ACTORS WHO HAVE PLAYED MOVIE LEADS IN DRAG

1. Charles Chaplin in *A Woman* (1915)
2. Jack Benny in *Charley's Aunt* (1941)
3. Joe E. Brown in *Shut My Big Mouth* (1942)
4. Lou Costello in *Lost in a Harem* (1944)
5. Ray Bolger in *Where's Charlie?* (1948)
6. Cary Grant in *I Was a Male War Bride* (1949)
7. Alec Guinness in *Kind Hearts and Coronets* (1949)
8. Jerry Lewis in *At War with the Army* (1950)
9. Jack Lemmon in *Some Like It Hot* (1959)
10. Tony Curtis in *Some Like It Hot* (1959)

10 ACTRESSES WHO HAVE PLAYED MOVIE LEADS IN DRAG

1. Miriam Hopkins in *She Loves Me Not* (1934)
2. Katharine Hepburn in *Sylvia Scarlett* (1935)
3. Louise Brooks in *Beggars of Life* (1936)
4. Shirley Temple in *Rebecca of Sunnybrook Farm* (1938)
5. Lupe Velez in *Honolulu Lu* (1939)
6. Marlene Dietrich in *Seven Sinners* (1940)
7. Merle Oberon in *A Song to Remember* (1945)
8. Maureen O'Hara in *At Sword's Point* (1952)
9. Doris Day in *Calamity Jane* (1953)
10. Raquel Welch in *Myra Breckenridge* (1970)

10 FAMOUS HOLLYWOOD PARTNERS

1. Sophia Loren and Marcello Mastroianni
2. Bud Abbott and Lou Costello
3. Dennis Morgan and Jack Carson
4. Fred Astaire and Ginger Rogers
5. Jeanette MacDonald and Nelson Eddy
6. Bing Crosby and Bob Hope
7. Dean Martin and Jerry Lewis
8. Diane Keaton and Woody Allen
9. Dan Dailey and Betty Grable
10. Elizabeth Taylor and Richard Burton

Marcello Mastroianni and Sophia Loren—a famous film partnership.

10 FAMOUS FOREIGN-BORN MOVIE ACTORS

1. Sean Connery (Edinburgh, Scotland)
2. Richard Burton (Pontrhydyfen, Wales)
3. Raymond Burr (New Westminster, Canada)
4. Desi Arnaz (Santiago, Cuba)
5. George Sanders (St. Petersburg, Russia)
6. Jacques Bergerac (Biarritz, France)
7. Ray Milland (Neath, Wales)
8. Paul Muni (Lemburg, Austria)
9. Peter Lorre (Rosenburg, Hungary)
10. Fernando Lamas (Buenos Aires, Argentina)

10 FAMOUS FOREIGN-BORN MOVIE ACTRESSES

1. Vivien Leigh (Darjeeling, India)
2. Ann-Margaret (Stockholm, Sweden)
3. Olivia de Havilland (Tokyo, Japan)
4. Joan Fontaine (Tokyo, Japan)
5. Pier Angeli (Cagilari, Sardinia)
6. Deborah Kerr (Helensburg, Scotland)
7. Greer Garson (County Down, Northern Ireland)
8. Audrey Hepburn (Brussels, Belgium)
9. Rita Moreno (Humacao, Puerto Rico)
10. Mary Pickford (Toronto, Canada)

Audrey Hepburn was born in Brussels, Belgium, adding to the list of Hollywood's famous foreign-born stars.

Ginger Rogers and Jean Phillips—Hollywood look-alikes.

10 HOLLYWOOD LOOK-ALIKES

1. Ginger Rogers and Jean Phillips
2. Paulette Goddard and Lynn Bari
3. Rudolph Valentino and Ricardo Cortez
4. Ronald Colman and Brian Aherne
5. Errol Flynn and Patrick Knowles
6. Ingrid Bergman and Viveca Lindfors
7. Lauren Bacall and Lizabeth Scott
8. Rita Hayworth and Mary Castle
9. Cary Grant and Gig Young
10. Rock Hudson and John Gavin

Lauren Bacall married Humphrey Bogart, but looked awfully like Lizabeth Scott.

5 STARS WHO HAVE PLAYED SECOND FIDDLE TO JOHN WAYNE

1. Claudette Colbert in *Without Reservations* (1946)
2. Oliver Hardy in *The Fighting Kentuckian* (1949)
3. Lauren Bacall in *Blood Alley* (1955)
4. Elsa Martinelli in *Hatari* (1962)
5. James Stewart in *The Shootist* (1976)

10 STARS WHO HAVE PLAYED ORIENTALS

1. Helen Hayes in *The Son-Daughter* (1932)
2. Luise Rainer in *The Good Earth* (1937)
3. Paul Muni in *The Good Earth* (1937)
4. Katharine Hepburn in *Dragon Seed* (1944)
5. Jean Simmons in *Black Narcissus* (1947)
6. Jennifer Jones in *Love Is a Many Splendored Thing* (1955)
7. Marlon Brando in *The Teahouse of the August Moon* (1956)
8. Robert Donat in *The Inn of the Sixth Happiness* (1958)
9. Mickey Rooney in *Breakfast at Tiffany's* (1961)
10. Shirley MacLaine in *The Gambit* (1966)

10 STARS WHO HAVE PLAYED INDIANS

1. Loretta Young in *Ramona* (1936)
2. Linda Darnell in *Buffalo Bill* (1944)
3. Boris Karloff in *Tap Roots* (1948)
4. Debra Paget in *Broken Arrow* (1950)
5. Charlton Heston in *The Savage* (1952)
6. Burt Lancaster in *Apache* (1954)
7. Jean Peters in *Apache* (1954)
8. Victor Mature in *Chief Crazy Horse* (1955)
9. Audrey Hepburn in *The Unforgiven* (1960)
10. Paul Newman in *Hombre* (1967)

Burt Lancaster—one of many Hollywood stars to have played the role of an Indian in westerns.

10 WHITE STARS WHO HAVE PLAYED IN BLACK FACE

1. Buster Keaton in *College* (1927)
2. Marion Davies in *Going Hollywood* (1933)
3. Fred Astaire in *Swing Time* (1936)
4. Judy Garland in *Babes in Arms* (1939)
5. Bing Crosby in *Dixie* (1943)
6. June Haver in *The Dolly Sisters* (1945)
7. Betty Gable in *The Dolly Sisters* (1945)
8. Larry Parks in *The Jolson Story* (1946)
9. Dan Dailey in *You're My Everything* (1949)
10. Gene Wilder in *Silver Streak* (1976)

Dan Dailey played in black face in You're My Everything.

10 MOVIE ACTORS WHO HAVE CREATED T.V. CHARACTERS

1. Raymond Burr: Ironside
2. Dennis Weaver: McCloud
3. William Conrad: Cannon
4. Mike Connors: Mannix
5. James Garner: Maverick
6. George Peppard: Banacek
7. Howard Duff: Dante
8. Roger Moore: Maverick
9. George Nader: Shannon
10. Gene Barry: Bat Masterson

8 ACTRESSES WHO HAVE PLAYED TEACHERS IN FILMS

1. Bette Davis in *The Corn Is Green* (1945)
2. Margaret Rutherford in *The Happiest Days of Your Life* (1950)
3. Jennifer Jones in *Good Morning, Miss Dove* (1955)
4. Shirley MacLaine in *Two Loves* (1961)
5. Sandy Dennis in *Up the Down Staircase* (1967)
6. Maggie Smith in *The Prime of Miss Jean Brodie* (1969)
7. Jane Wyman in *The Failing of Raymond* (1971)
8. Diane Keaton in *Looking for Mr. Goodbar* (1977)

5 ACTORS WHO HAVE PLAYED TEACHERS IN FILMS

1. Emil Jannings in *The Blue Angel* (1930)
2. Robert Donat in *Goodbye Mr. Chips* (1939)
3. Glenn Ford in *The Blackboard Jungle* (1955)
4. Sidney Poitier in *To Sir with Love* (1967)

10 ACTRESSES WHO HAVE PLAYED DOMESTICS IN FILMS

1. Joan Crawford in *A Woman's Face* (1941)
2. Angela Lansbury in *Gaslight* (1944)
3. Jane Wyman in *Make Your Own Bed* (1944)
4. Greer Garson in *The Valley of Decision* (1945)
5. Jennifer Jones in *Cluny Brown* (1946)
6. Loretta Young in *The Farmer's Daughter* (1947)
7. Thelma Ritter in *All About Eve* (1950)
8. Bette Davis in *The Nanny* (1965)
9. Paulette Goddard in *Diary of a Chambermaid* (1965)
10. Joan Fontaine in *Jane Eyre* (1971)

10 ACTORS WHO HAVE PLAYED DOMESTICS IN FILMS

1. Charles Laughton in *Ruggles of Red Gap* (1935)
2. Basil Rathbone in *Private Number* (1936)
3. Alan Mowbray in *Topper* (1937)
4. Charles Boyer in *Tovarich* (1937)
5. William Powell in *The Baroness and the Butler* (1938)
6. Henry Fonda in *Drums Along the Mohawk* (1939)
7. Jack Carson in *Make Your Own Bed* (1944)
8. Bob Hope in *Fancy Pants* (1950)
9. David Niven in *My Man Godfrey* (1957)
10. Dirk Bogarde in *The Servant* (1963)

10 FAMOUS ACTRESSES WHO HAVE PLAYED OTHER SHOW BUSINESS PERSONALITIES ON THE SCREEN

1. Alice Faye as Lillian Russell in *Lillian Russell* (1940)
2. June Haver as Marilyn Miller in *Look for the Silver Lining* (1949)
3. Betty Hutton as Blossom Seeley in *Somebody Loves Me* (1952)
4. Mitzi Gaynor as Eva Tanguay in *The Helen Morgan Story* (1957)
5. Kathryn Grayson as Grace Moore in *So This Is Love* (1953)
6. Eleanor Parker as Marjorie Lawrence in *Interrupted Melody* (1955)
7. Doris Day as Ruth Etting in *Love Me or Leave Me* (1955)
8. Susan Hayward as Lillian Roth in *I'll Cry Tomorrow* (1955)

9. Ann Blyth as Helen Morgan in *The Helen Morgan Story* (1957)

10. Barbra Streisand as Fanny Brice in *Funny Girl* (1968) and *Funny Lady* (1975)

10 FAMOUS ACTORS WHO HAVE PLAYED OTHER SHOWBUSINESS PERSONALITIES ON THE SCREEN

1. Fred Astaire as Vernon Castle in *The Story of Vernon and Irene Castle* (1939)

2. James Cagney as George M. Cohan in *Yankee Doodle Dandy* (1942)

3. Larry Parks as Al Jolson in *The Jolson Story* (1946)

4. Mario Lanza as Enrico Caruso in *The Great Caruso* (1951)

5. Clifton Webb as John Philip Sousa in *Stars and Stripes Forever* (1952)

6. Tony Curtis as Harry Houdini in *Houdini* (1953)

7. James Stewart as Glenn Miller in *The Glenn Miller Story* (1954)

8. Steve Allen as Benny Goodman in *The Benny Goodman Story* (1955)

9. Bob Hope as Eddie Foy in *The Seven Little Foys* (1955)

10. Richard Burton as Edwin Booth in *Prince of Players* (1955)

10 FAMOUS ACTORS WHO HAVE PLAYED THE TITLE ROLE IN ADVENTURE FILMS

1. Mickey Rooney in *Adventures of Huckleberry Finn* (1932)

2. Gary Cooper in *Adventures of Marco Polo* (1937)

Doris Day was one of many actresses who played other show-business personalities on the screen. In 1955 she starred in the life of Ruth Etting in Love Me or Leave Me.

3. Errol Flynn in *Adventures of Robin Hood* (1938)

4. Tommy Kelly in *Adventures of Tom Sawyer* (1938)

5. Basil Rathbone in *Adventures of Sherlock Holmes* (1939)

6. Glenn Ford in *Adventures of Martin Eden* (1942)

7. Robert Donat in *Adventures of Tartu* (1943)

8. Fredric March in *Adventures of Mark Twain* (1944)

9. Dan O'Herlihy in *Adventures of Robinson Crusoe* (1954)

10. John Derek in *Adventures of Haji Baba* (1954)

10 ACTORS WHO HAVE PLAYED KINGS IN MOVIES

1. Humphrey Bogart in *King of the Underworld* (1939)

2. Rex Harrison in *Anna and the King of Siam* (1946)

3. Tyrone Power in *King of the Khyber Rifles* (1953)

4. George Sanders in *King Richard and the Crusades* (1954)

5. Clark Gable in *The King and Four Queens* (1956)

6. Yul Brynner in *The King and I* (1956)

7. Elvis Presley in *King Creole* (1958)

8. George Segal in *King Rat* (1965)

9. Richard Burton in *Anne of the Thousand Days* (1969)

10. Paul Scofield in *King Lear* (1971)

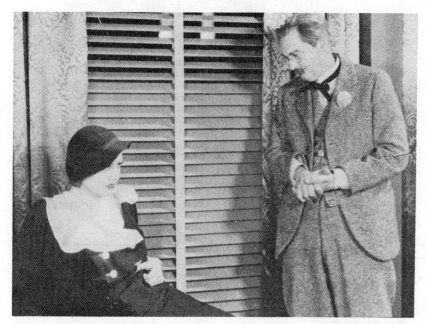

Joan Crawford and Lionel Barrymore in Grand Hotel *(1932). The very young Crawford was breathtakingly beautiful in her role as an ambitious secretary-stenographer.*

10 ACTRESSES WHO HAVE PLAYED SECRETARIES IN FILMS

1. Claudette Colbert in *Secrets of a Secretary* (1931)
2. Joan Crawford in *Grand Hotel* (1932)
3. Jean Harlow in *Wife vs. Secretary* (1936)
4. Ann Sothern in *Trade Winds* (1938)
5. Ginger Rogers in *My Dear Secretary* (1948) and in *Kitty Foyle* (1940
6. Rosalind Russell in *Hired Wife* (1940)
7. Olivia de Havilland in *Government Girl* (1943)
8. Jane Wyman in *Crime by Night* (1944)
9. Lana Turner in *Weekend at the Waldorf* (1945)
10. Marilyn Monroe in *My Friend Irma* (1949)

John Wayne, the former University of Southern California football hero, was another famous athlete who became a movie star.

10 FAMOUS JAMES CAGNEY MOVIES

1. *Smart Money* (1931)
2. *Lady Killer* (1933)
3. *Footlight Parade* (1933)
4. *Hard to Handle* (1933)
5. *Angels with Dirty Faces* (1938)
6. *The Strawberry Blonde* (1941)
7. *Yankee Doodle Dandy* (1942)
8. *Johnny Come Lately* (1943)
9. *Thirteen Rue Madeleine* (1946)
10. *Never Steal Anything Small* (1958)

10 FAMOUS ATHLETES WHO BECAME MOVIE STARS

1. John Wayne—University of Southern California football star
2. Alan Ladd—United States diving champion
3. Archie Moore—world light-heavyweight boxing champion
4. Chuck Connors—Brooklyn Dodgers' first baseman
5. Eleanor Holm—Olympic swimming champion (backstroke)
6. Johnny Weissmuller—Olympic swimming champion (free-style)
7. Sonja Henie—Olympic figure skating champion
8. Andy Devine—Santa Clara University football hero
9. Bob Mathias—Olympic decathlon champion
10. Max Barr—World heavyweight boxing champion

10 FAMOUS ACTRESSES WHO HAVE PLAYED MURDERESSES IN FILMS

1. Mae West in *She Done Him Wrong* (1933)
2. Bette Davis in *The Letter* (1940)
3. Rosalind Russell in *The Velvet Touch* (1948)
4. Ginger Rogers in *Black Widow* (1954)
5. Patty McCormack in *The Bad Seed* (1956)
6. Faye Dunaway in *Bonnie and Clyde* (1967)
7. Jacqueline Bissett in *Murder on the Orient Express* (1974)
8. Sissy Spacek in *Carrie* (1967)
9. Mia Farrow in *Death on the Nile* (1977)
10. Dyan Cannon in *Heaven Can Wait* (1978)

10 FAMOUS ACTORS WHO HAVE PLAYED MURDERERS IN FILMS

1. Spencer Tracy in *The Murder Man* (1935)
2. John Barrymore in *Night Club Scandal* (1937)
3. Clifton Webb in *Laura* (1944)
4. Charles Boyer in *Gaslight* (1944)
5. Barry Fitzgerald in *And Then There Were None* (1945)
6. Farley Granger in *Rope* (1948)
7. Tyrone Power in *Witness for the Prosecution* (1957)
8. Anthony Perkins in *Psycho* (1960)
9. Rex Harrison in *The Honey Pot* (1967)
10. Tony Curtis in *The Boston Strangler* (1968)

Jacqueline Bissett played an unlikely murderess in Murder on the Orient Express *(1974).*

10 MORE FAMOUS ACTORS WHO HAVE PLAYED MURDERERS IN FILMS

1. James Stewart in *After the Thin Man* (1936)
2. George Brent in *The Spiral Staircase* (1946)
3. Robert Ryan in *Crossfire* (1947)
4. Richard Todd in *Stage Fright* (1950)
5. Raymond Burr in *Rear Window* (1954)
6. Ray Milland in *Dial M for Murder* (1954)
7. Kirk Douglas in *The List of Adrian Messenger* (1963)
8. Barry Foster in *Frenzy* (1972)
9. Edward Fox in *Day of the Jackal* (1973)
10. Robert DeNiro in *The Godfather, Part II* (1974)

10 FAMOUS MOVIE STARS WHO HAVE PLAYED SECOND FIDDLE TO SHIRLEY TEMPLE IN THE MOVIES

1. Jack McCrae in *Our Little Girl* (1935)
2. Lionel Barrymore in *The Little Colonel* (1935)
3. Jack Haley in *Poor Little Rich Girl* (1936)
4. Frank Morgan in *Dimples* (1936)
5. George Murphy in *Little Miss Broadway* (1938)
6. Anita Louise in *The Little Princess* (1939)
7. Margaret Lockwood in *Susannah of the Mounties* (1939)
8. Ronald Reagan in *That Hagen Girl* (1947)
9. Franchot Tone in *Honeymoon* (1947)
10. Clifton Webb in *Mr. Belvedere Goes to College* (1949)

Elizabeth Taylor—one of seven famous Hollywood actresses to have played Cleopatra.

7 ACTRESSES WHO HAVE PLAYED CLEOPATRA

1. Helen Gardner (1911)
2. Theda Bara (1917)
3. Claudette Colbert (1934)
4. Vivien Leigh (1945)
5. Amanda Barrie (1963)
6. Elizabeth Taylor (1963)
7. Hildegarde Neil (1972)

8 MOVIE ACTORS WHO HAVE PLAYED NAPOLEON

1. Abel Gance (1925) in *Napoleon*
2. Charles Boyer (1937) in *Marie Walewska*

108

3. Herbert Lom (1941) in *The Young Mr. Pitt*
4. Arnold Moss (1949) in *The Black Book*
5. Marlon Brando (1954) in *Desirée*
6. Herbert Lom (1956) in *War and Peace*
7. Pierre Mondy (1960) in *Austerlitz*
8. Rod Steiger (1970) in *Waterloo*

10 MOVIE STARS WHO HAVE PLAYED NUNS

1. Jennifer Jones in *The Song of Bernadette* (1943)
2. Rosalind Russell in *Sister Kenny* (1946)
3. Loretta Young in *Come to the Stable* (1949)
4. Celeste Holm in *Come to the Stable* (1949)
5. Deborah Kerr in *Heaven Knows, Mr. Allison* (1956)
6. Audrey Hepburn in *The Nun's Story* (1956)
7. Lilli Palmer in *Conspiracy of Hearts* (1960)
8. Debbie Reynolds in *The Singing Nun* (1966)
9. Vanessa Redgrave in *The Devils* (1971)
10. Shirley MacLaine in *Two Mules for Sister Sara* (1971)

10 FAMOUS CHILD STARS

1. Shirley Temple
2. Margaret O'Brien
3. Tatum O'Neal
4. Jodie Foster
5. Roddy McDowall
6. Jackie Coogen
7. Patty Duke
8. Hayley Mills
9. Patty McCormack
10. Freddie Bartholomew

10 LEADING MEN WHO HAVE PLAYED SECOND FIDDLE TO JUDY GARLAND

1. Buddy Ebsen in *Pigskin Parade* (1936)
2. Jack Haley and Ray Bolger in *The Wizard of Oz* (1939)
3. Mickey Rooney first in *Babes in Arms* (1939)
4. Tom Drake in *Meet Me in St. Louis* (1944)
5. Gene Kelly in *The Pirate* (1947)
6. Fred Astaire in *Easter Parade* (1948)
7. Van Johnson in *In the Good Old Summertime* (1949)
8. James Mason in *A Star Is Born* (1954)
9. Burt Lancaster in *A Child Is Waiting* (1963)
10. Dirk Bogarde in *I Could Go on Singing* (1963)

10 MOVIE STARS WHO HAVE PLAYED PRIESTS

1. Spencer Tracy in *The Men of Boys' Town* (1941)
2. Bing Crosby in *Going My Way* (1944)
3. Gregory Peck in *The Keys of the Kingdom* (1944)
4. Henry Fonda in *The Fugitive* (1947)
5. Frank Sinatra in *The Miracle of the Bells* (1948)
6. Montgomery Clift in *I Confess* (1953)
7. Alec Guinness in *Father Brown* (1954)
8. Karl Malden in *On the Waterfront* (1954)
9. John Mills in *The Singer Not the Song* (1960)
10. Richard Burton in *The Night of the Iguana* (1964)

Fred Astaire played second fiddle to Judy Garland in Easter Parade *(1948).*

Jodie Foster—another rising Hollywood child star.

Ava Gardner with director John Ford. The turbulent star played opposite Clark Gable in Mogambo *(1953).*

11 ACTRESSES WHO HAVE PLAYED SECOND FIDDLE TO CLARK GABLE

1. Greta Garbo in *Susan Lenox—Her Fall and Rise* (1931)
2. Norma Shearer in *Strange Interlude* (1932)
3. Claudette Colbert in *It Happened One Night* (1934)
4. Jeanette MacDonald in *San Francisco* (1936)
5. Joan Crawford in *Love on the Run* (1937)
6. Vivien Leigh in *Gone with the Wind* (1939)
7. Lana Turner in *Honky Tonk* (1941)
8. Alexis Smith in *Any Number Can Play* (1949)
9. Ava Gardner in *Mogambo* (1953)
10. Sophia Loren in *It Started in Naples* (1959)
11. Marilyn Monroe in *The Misfits* (1961)

3
THE DIRECTORS

10 QUOTATIONS BY PEOPLE WHO HELPED BUILD HOLLYWOOD

1. "There were times my pants were so thin I could sit on a dime and know if it was heads or tails."

    Spencer Tracy, referring to his early days in show business

2. "Beaulah, peel me a grape."

    Mae West

3. "They don't make faces like that any more."

    Gloria Swanson, in *Sunset Boulevard*

4. "Gentlemen—include me out."

    Samuel Goldwyn

5. "I am too tragic by nature to play Hamlet. Only a great comedian can act him."

    Charlie Chaplin

6. "I can answer you in two words—Im Possible!"

    Samuel Goldwyn

7. "I have a face like the behind of an elephant."

    Charles Laughton

8. "I don't like security. I want to change and meet new people."

    Ingrid Bergman, just before she met Roberto Rossellini

9. "We had principles. You *had* to stay up late and get drunk, and all our members were against the P.T.A."

    Lauren Bacall, referring to the Kennedy-era Rat Pack

10. "You say I can't delegate. The point is, I don't want to."

    David O. Selznick

THE 10 BEST DIRECTORS

1. Charles Chaplin
2. Sergei Eisenstein
3. René Clair
4. Vittorio De Sica
5. D. W. Griffith

6. John Ford
7. Jean Renoir
8. Carl Dreyer
9. Erich Von Stroheim
10. Vsevolod Pudovkin

1958 Brussels World Fair Survey

Charlie Chaplin was voted one of the ten best directors in a 1958 Brussels World Fair Survey.

10 FAMOUS DIRECTORS WHO HAVE ALSO APPEARED IN MOVIES

1. Charles Chaplin— *The Gold Rush* (1923) among many others
2. Jean Renoir— *La Règle du Jeu* (1939)
3. John Huston— *The Treasure of Sierra Madre* (1947)
4. Cecil B. de Mille— *Sunset Boulevard* (1950). He played himself.
5. Ingmar Bergman— *Waiting Women* (1952)
6. Otto Preminger— *Stalag 17* (1953)
7. Alfred Hitchcock— *To Catch a Thief* (1955) and many others
8. Jules Dassin— *Never on Sunday* (1963)
9. Tony Richardson— *Tom Jones* (1963)
10. Roman Polanski— *The Magic Christian* (1969)

17 MOVIE STARS WHO HAVE ALSO DIRECTED FILMS

1. Charles Chaplin— *A Countess from Hong Kong* (1967), and all his other feature films except *A Woman of Paris* (1923)
2. Orson Welles— *Citizen Kane* (1941) and others
3. Clint Eastwood— *Play Misty for Me* (1971)
4. Marlon Brando— *One-Eyed Jacks* (1960)
5. Gene Kelly— *Hello Dolly* (1969) and others
6. Paul Newman— *Rachel Rachel* (1968) and *Sometimes a Great Notion* (1971)
7. Peter Ustinov— *Hammersmith Is Out* (1972) and others
8. Laurence Olivier— *The Prince and the Showgirl* (1958)
9. Bob Fosse— *Cabaret* (1972) and others
10. John Wayne— *The Alamo* (1960) and *The Green Berets* (1968)

A masterful director, Alfred Hitchock usually appeared in his own movies.

11. Charlton Heston— *Antony and Cleopatra* (1973)

12. Jack Lemmon— *Kotch* (1971)

13. José Ferrer— *The Great Man* (1956)

14. Walter Matthau— *The Gangster Story* (1960)

15. Ray Milland— *A Man Alone* (1955)

16. Ralph Richardson— *Murder on Monday* (1953)

17. Woody Allen—notably *Sleeper* (1973), *Annie Hall* (1977), *Interiors* (1978), and *Manhattan* (1979)

ELIA KAZAN'S 10 FAVORITE MOVIES

1. *Battleship Potemkin* (Eisenstein, 1925)

2. *Aerograd* (Dovzhenko)

3. *The Gold Rush* (Chaplin, 1925)

4. *Flesh and the Devil* (Brown, 1927)

5. *Open City* (Rossellini, 1946)

6. *The Bicycle Thief* (De Sica, 1949)

7. *Shoulder Arms* (Chaplin, 1918)

8. *Target for Tonight* (Watt)

9. *Le Femme du Boulanger* (Pagnol)

10. *Marius, Fanny, Cesar* (Pagnol)

1952 Cinémathèque Belgique Survey

ORSON WELLES'S 10 FAVORITE MOVIES

1. *City Lights* (1931)
2. *Greed* (1924)
3. *Intolerance* (1916)
4. *Nanook* (1922)
5. *Sciuscia* (De Sica)
6. *The Battleship Potemkin* (1925)
7. *La Femme du Boulanger* (Pagnol)
8. *La Grande Illusion* (1937)
9. *Stagecoach* (1939)
10. *Our Daily Bread* (Vidor 1934)

1952 Cinémathèque Belgique Survey

KING VIDOR'S 10 FAVORITE MOVIES

1. *Intolerance* (1916)
2. *Sunrise* (1927)
3. *Der Ietzte Mann* (Murnau)
4. *The Big Parade* (Vidor, 1925)
5. *Brief Encounter* (1946)
6. *Red Shoes* (1948)
7. *Open City* (1946)
8. *City Lights* (1931)
9. *Citizen Kane* (1941)
10. *The Best Years of Our Lives* (1946)

1952 Cinémathèque Belgique Survey

VITTORIO DE SICA'S 10 FAVORITE MOVIES

1. *Man of Aran* (1934)
2. *The Kid* (1921)
3. *La Chienne* (Renoir)
4. *Le Million* (1930)
5. *L'Atalante*
6. *Kameradschaft* (Pabst)
7. *Storm Over Asia*
8. *The Battleship Potemkin* (1925)
9. *Hallelujah!* (1929)
10. *La Kemesse Heroique* (Feyder)

1952 Cinémathèque Belgique Survey

PETER BOGDANOVICH'S 10 FAVORITE MOVIES

1. *Only Angels Have Wings* (1939)
2. *Young Mr. Lincoln* (1939)
3. *The Magnificent Ambersons* (1942)
4. *Red River* (1948)
5. *She Wore a Yellow Ribbon* (1949)
6. *The Searchers* (1956)
7. *Rio Bravo* (1959)
8. *Touch of Evil* (1958)
9. *Vertigo* (1958)
10. *North by Northwest* (1959)

1972 *Sight and Sound* Survey

121

"*Give me a couple of pages of the Bible and I'll give you a picture.*"

Cecil B. De Mille

4
THE STUDIOS

10 REVEALING QUOTATIONS MADE IN THE STUDIOS

1. "I don't have ulcers—I give them."
   Harry Cohn

2. "Drama is life with the dull bits left out."
   Alfred Hitchcock

3. "Give me a couple of pages of the Bible and I'll give you a picture."
   Cecil B. De Mille

4. "I started at the top and worked down."
   Orson Welles

5. "A man should control his life. Mine is controlling me."
   Rudolph Valentino, in the year of his death, 1926

6. "The monster was the best friend I ever had."
   Boris Karloff

7. "I was never interested in doing anything that was easy."
   Bette Davis

8. "I have never gone after honors instead of dollars. But I have understood the relationship between them."
   David O. Selznick

9. "The cinema has bred a race of giant popcorn-eating rats."
   Vincent Price

10. "Chaplin is the one man in the world I want to meet."
    Lenin

Jaws is the second-biggest moneymaking film of all time. The topic proved so popular that even its sequel, Jaws II, *is among the eighteen biggest moneymakers.*

THE 10 TOP MONEYMAKING FILMS OF ALL TIME

1. *Star Wars* (1977)
2. *Jaws* (1975)
3. *The Godfather* (1972)
4. *Grease* (1978)
5. *The Exorcist* (1973)
6. *The Sound of Music* (1965)
7. *The Sting* (1973)
8. *Close Encounters of the Third Kind* (1977)
9. *Gone With the Wind* (1939)
10. *Saturday Night Fever* (1977)

Variety, January 1979

John Travolta and Karen Lynn Gorney dance to the explosive beat in Saturday Night Fever— *the tenth-biggest moneymaking film of all time.*

Alec Guinness won an Oscar for best supporting actor in Star Wars *(1977). So far it has been the top moneymaking film of all time.*

THE SECOND 10 TOP MONEYMAKING FILMS OF ALL TIME

1. *One Flew Over the Cuckoo's Nest* (1975)
2. *Smokey and the Bandit* (1977)
3. *American Graffiti* (1973)
4. *Rocky* (1976)
5. *National Lampoon Animal House* (1978)
6. *Love Story* (1970)
7. *Towering Inferno* (1975)
8. *Jaws II* (1978)
9. *The Graduate* (1968)
10. *Doctor Zhivago* (1965)

Variety, January 1979

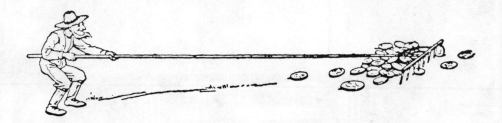

THE 8 MOST SUCCESSFUL U.S. MOTION PICTURE STUDIOS *

1. Buena Vista/Disney
2. Columbia Pictures
3. Metro-Goldwyn-Mayer
4. Paramount Pictures
5. Twentieth-Century Fox

6. United Artists
7. Universal Studios
8. Warner Brothers

*Listed Alphabetically

The Economist

Greta Garbo was under contract to MGM in 1930. Over the years MGM has remained one of the most successful Holly-wood motion picture studios.

BUENA VISTA/DISNEY'S TOP 10 MONEYMAKING FILMS

1. *Mary Poppins* (1964)
2. *Snow White* (1937)
3. *The Love Bug* (1969)
4. *Swiss Family Robinson* (1960)
5. *Bambi* (1942)
6. *Herbie Rides Again* (1974)
7. *The Apple Dumpling Gang* (1975)
8. *Peter Pan* (1953)
9. *1001 Dalmatians* (1961)
10. *Pinocchio* (1940)

Variety, January 1979

UNITED ARTISTS' TOP 10 MONEYMAKING FILMS

1. *One Flew Over the Cuckoo's Nest* (1975)
2. *Rocky* (1976)
3. *Fiddler on the Roof* (1971)
4. *Thunderball* (1965)
5. *Revenge of the Pink Panther* (1978)
6. *Around the World in 80 Days* (1956)
7. *Goldfinger* (1964)
8. *The Spy Who Loved Me* (1977)
9. *A Bridge Too Far* (1977)
10. *It's a Mad, Mad, Mad, Mad, World* (1963)

Variety, January 1979

COLUMBIA PICTURES' TOP 10 MONEYMAKING FILMS

1. *Close Encounters of the Third Kind* (1977)
2. *The Deep* (1977)
3. *Funny Girl* (1968)
4. *Shampoo* (1975)
5. *Murder by Death* (1976)
6. *The Cheap Detective* (1978)
7. *To Sir With Love* (1967)
8. *Funny Lady* (1975)
9. *The Bridge on the River Kwai* (1957)
10. *The Way We Were* (1973)

Variety, January 1979

METRO GOLDWYN MAYER'S TOP 10 MONEYMAKING FILMS

1. *Gone With the Wind* (1939)
2. *Doctor Zhivago* (1965)
3. *Ben-Hur* (1959)
4. *2001: A Space Odyssey* (1968)
5. *The Dirty Dozen* (1967)
6. *Ryan's Daughter* (1970)
7. *Quo Vadis* (1951)
8. *How the West Was Won* (1962) (Made with Cinerama)
9. *That's Entertainment* (1974) (released by U.A.)
10. *Mutiny on the Bounty* (1962)

Variety, January 1979

PARAMOUNT PICTURES' TOP 10 MONEYMAKING FILMS

1. *The Godfather* (1972)
2. *Grease* (1978)
3. *Saturday Night Fever* (1977)
4. *Love Story* (1970)
5. *The Ten Commandments* (1956)
6. *Heaven Can Wait* (1978)
7. *King Kong* (1976)
8. *The Godfather Part II* (1974)
9. *The Bad News Bears* (1976)
10. *The Longest Yard* (1974)

Variety, January 1979

20TH CENTURY FOX'S TOP 10 MONEYMAKING FILMS

1. *Star Wars* (1977)
2. *The Sound of Music* (1965)
3. *Towering Inferno* (1973) (made with Warner Brothers)
4. *Butch Cassidy and the Sundance Kid* (1969)
5. *The Poseidon Adventure* (1972)
6. *M*A*S*H** (1970)
7. *Young Frankenstein* (1975)
8. *Silver Streak* (1976)
9. *Patton* (1970)
10. *The French Connection* (1971)

Variety, January 1979

Dick van Dyke starred in Mary Poppins— *one of Buena Vista/ Disney's top 10 moneymaking films.*

UNIVERSAL STUDIOS' TOP 10 MONEYMAKING FILMS

1. *Jaws* (1975)
2. *The Sting* (1973)
3. *Smokey and the Bandit* (1977)
4. *American Graffiti* (1973)
5. *National Lampoon Animal House* (1978)
6. *Jaws II* (1978)
7. *Airport* (1970)
8. *Earthquake* (1974)
9. *Midway* (1976)
10. *The Other Side of the Mountain* (1975)

Variety, January 1979

WARNER BROTHERS' TOP 10 MONEYMAKING FILMS

1. *The Exorcist* (1973)
2. *The Towering Inferno* (1975) (made with 20th Century Fox)
3. *The Goodbye Girl* (1977)
4. *Blazing Saddles* (1974)
5. *A Star Is Born* (1976)
6. *Billy Jack* (1971)
7. *Hooper* (1978)
8. *Oh, God* (1977)
9. *All the President's Men* (1976)
10. *Trial of Billy Jack* (1974)

Variety, January 1979

11 PRINCIPLES OF THE CODE OF SELF REGULATION OF THE MOTION PICTURE ASSOCIATION

1. The basic dignity and value of human life shall be respected and upheld. Restraint shall be exercised in portraying the taking of life.
2. Evil, sin, crime, and wrong-doing shall not be justified.
3. Special restraint shall be exercised in portraying criminal or anti-social activities in which minors participate or are involved.
4. Detailed and protracted acts of brutality, cruelty, physical violence, torture, and abuse shall not be presented.
5. Indecent or undue exposure of the human body shall not be presented.
6. Illicit sex relationships shall not be justified. Intimate sex

scenes violating common standards of decency shall not be portrayed.

7. Restraint and care shall be exercised in presentations dealing with sex aberrations.

8. Obscene speech, gestures, or movements shall not be presented. Undue profanity shall not be permitted.

9. Religion shall not be demeaned.

10. Words or symbols contemptuous of racial, religious, or national groups shall not be used so as to incite bigotry or hatred.

11. Excessive cruelty to animals shall not be portrayed and animals shall not be treated inhumanely.

Motion Picture Association of America

THE MOST UNUSUAL SPECIAL EFFECT

In the film *The Scent of Mystery* Mike Todd, Jr., in 1960, introduced 'Smell-o-Vision'—and the claim that the film was "the first movie to stink on purpose." Fifty-two different essences were dispensed through scent vents behind each theatre seat, but despite millions of dollars spent on promotion, the process was a theatrical and financial disaster.

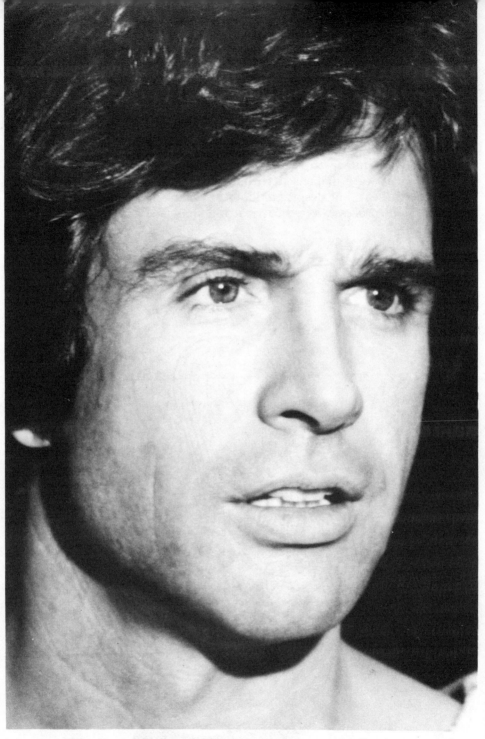

"Movies are fun but they're not a cure for cancer."
Warren Beatty

136

5
CONTROVERSIAL TOPICS

10 QUOTATIONS ABOUT HOLLYWOOD

1. "They've great respect for the dead in Hollywood, but none for the living."
   Errol Flynn

2. "Two of the cruelest, most primitive punishments our town deals out to those who fall from favor are the empty mailbox and the silent telephone."
   Hedda Hopper

3. "It's a great place to live—if you're an orange."
   Fred Allen

4. "Hollywood is a carnival where there are no concessions."
   Wilson Mizner

5. "Ten million dollars worth of intricate and ingenious machinery functioning elaborately to put skin on baloney."
   George Jean Nathan

6. "It's somehow symbolic of Hollywood that Tara was just a façade, with no rooms inside."
   David O. Selznick

7. "Hollywood hostesses never invited columnists to their parties. Once you did you could never leave them off your list. They would crucify you."
   Ray Milland, *Wide-Eyed in Babylon*

8. "Hollywood is a sewer—with service from the Ritz Carlton.
   Wilson Mizner

9. "Movies are fun, but they're not a cure for cancer."
   Warren Beatty

10. "If you want art, don't mess around with movies. Buy a Picasso."
    Michael Winner

10 MOVIES ABOUT HOMOSEXUALITY

1. *Tea and Sympathy* (1956)

    Robert Anderson's play is brought to the screen—the story of a prep school boy (John Kerr) who falls in love with his master's wife, beautifully acted by Deborah Kerr. The play's homosexual issues are, however, skirted.

2. *Cat on a Hot Tin Roof* (1958)

    Elizabeth Taylor vies for Paul Newman's love while he mourns the suicide of his football-playing friend.

3. *Suddenly, Last Summer* (1959)

    Montgomery Clift uses Elizabeth Taylor as his bait for the young boys he needs to satisfy his closet homosexuality.

4. *Spartacus* (1960)

    An implied relationship between Laurence Olivier and his servant Tony Curtis.

5. *Victim* (1961)

    Dirk Bogarde plays a trapped ambivalent barrister; Peter McEnery a young man driven to suicide.

6. *The Servant* (1963)

    Dirk Bogarde gives a superb performance as a corrupt manservant who becomes the master of employer James Fox.

7. *Inside Daisy Clover* (1966)

    Robert Redford plays a young actor who runs out on Natalie Wood on their wedding night.

8. *Reflections in a Golden Eye* (1967)

    Marlon Brando is an army officer in pursuit of an enlisted man who is more interested in Brando's wife, Elizabeth Taylor, than in him.

9. *The Lion in Winter* (1968)

    Richard Burton plays the future King Richard, allegedly a homosexual.

10. *Cabaret* (1972)

    Michael York plays an unhappy but sympathetic Englishman who cannot quite make it with Liza Minnelli.

Marlon Brando played a homosexual army officer in Reflections in a Golden Eye *(1967).*

Liza Minnelli won an Oscar for her role in Cabaret (1972)—
*one of the first movies to openly portray homosexuality and
anti-Semitism.*

Frank Sinatra was unforgettable as an alcoholic in The Joker Is Wild *(1957). One of the songs from the film, "All the Way," won an Oscar.*

10 MOVIE ALCOHOLICS

1. Ray Milland in *The Lost Weekend* (1945)
2. Burt Lancaster in *Come Back Little Sheba* (1952)
3. Bing Crosby in *The Country Girl* (1954)
4. Susan Hayward in *I'll Cry Tomorrow* (1956)
5. Ann Blyth in *The Helen Morgan Story* (1957)
6. Frank Sinatra in *The Joker Is Wild* (1958)

7. Paul Newman in *Cat on a Hot Tin Roof* (1958)

8. Gregory Peck in *Beloved Infidel* (1959)

9. Lee Remick in *Days of Wine and Roses* (1962)

10. Lee Marvin in *Cat Ballou* (1965)

10 POLITICIANS PORTRAYED IN MOVIES

1. Lord Nelson, played by Laurence Olivier in *That Hamilton Woman* (1942) and by Cedric Hardwicke in *Nelson* (1926).

2. Woodrow Wilson played by Alexander Knox in *Wilson* (1944).

3. Andrew Jackson, played by Charlton Heston in *The President's Lady* (1953).

4. William Jennings Bryan, played by Cedric March in *Inherit the Wind* (1960).

5. Franklin Delano Roosevelt, played by Ralph Bellamy in *Sunrise at Campobello* (1960).

6. Adolf Hitler, played by Richard Basehart in *Hitler* (1961).

7. John F. Kennedy, played by Cliff Robertson in *PT 109* (1963).

8. William Gladstone, played by Ralph Richardson in *Khartoum* (1966).

9. The Duke of Wellington, played by Christopher Plummer in *Waterloo* (1969).

10. Winston Churchill, played by John Ward in *Young Winston* (1972).

10 MOVIES ABOUT THE DESTRUCTION OF THE WORLD

1. *Seven Days to Noon* (1950)

2. *When Worlds Collide* (1951)

142

3. *The War of the Worlds* (1953)

4. *Invaders from Mars* (1954)

5. *The Invasion of the Body Snatchers* (1956)

6. *The 27th Day* (1957)

7. *Quaternass and the Pit* (1957)

8. *On the Beach* (1959)

9. *The Day the Earth Caught Fire* (1962)

10. *Dr. Strangelove* (1963)

10 FAMOUS WAR MOVIES

1. *Stalag 17* (1953)

2. *From Here to Eternity* (1953)

3. *Mr. Roberts* (1955)

4. *The Bridge on the River Kwai* (1957)

5. *The Young Lions* (1958)

6. *The Longest Day* (1962)

7. *Patton* (1969)

8. *M*A*S*H** (1970)

9. *The Deer Hunter* (1978)

10. *Apocalypse Now* (1979)

10 FAMOUS "RACKET" FILMS

1. *The Wet Parade* (1932)
   Liquor

2. *The Big Sleep* (1946)
   Gambling

3. *The Third Man* (1949)
   The Black Market

4. *All the King's Men* (1950)
   Politics

Robert DeNiro, probably the most gifted and versatile actor today, won an Oscar for his portrayal of the young Mafia patriarch in The Godfather/Part II *(1974).*

5. *On the Waterfront* (1954)
   Organized Labor
6. *The Harder They Fall* (1956)
   Boxing
7. *The French Connection* (1971)
   Drugs and Organized Crime
8. *The Godfather* (1972)
   The Mafia
9. *Chinatown* (1974)
   Police Corruption
10. *Taxi Driver* (1976)
    Prostitution

10 FAMOUS "BLACK" COMEDIES

1. *Arsenic and Old Lace* (1944)
   Murder and evil among little old ladies
2. *The Loved One* (1965)
   A bizarre treatment of the American way of death
3. *The Anniversary* (1967)
   Bette Davis makes fun of mother, love, and apple pie
4. *No Way to Treat a Lady* (1968)
   A light treatment of the Oedipus complex and murder
5. *M*A*S*H** (1970)
   Lampooning medicine, war, and the army
6. *The Best of Friends* (1971)
   An exposé of the medical profession
7. *Black Flowers for the Bride* (1971)
   Family life among the German aristocracy is examined under a very strong light
8. *Loot* (1971)
   The subject is human relationships
9. *The Hospital* (1972)
   Impotence, death, and murder are lightly treated
10. *A Day in the Death of Joe Egg* (1972)
    Living and coping with a spastic child

Orson Welles' role in Citizen Kane *(1941) bore a striking resemblance to that of the newspaper tycoon William Randolph Hearst. The film is considered to be one of the best ever made.*

10 FAMOUS MOVIES A CLEF

1. *Citizen Kane* (1941)

   The story of a newspaper publisher's rise to power. Orson Welles, who also directed the film, plays the title role which bears a striking resemblance to Randolph Hearst.

2. *Caught* (1949)

Robert Ryan plays Howard Hughes in this compelling movie about a young girl who marries a powerful multi-millionaire.

3. *All About Eve* (1950)

Bette Davis gives a masterful performance as an aging star, reputedly Tallulah Bankhead. The movie won a handful of Oscars, including Best Picture, Best Direction, Best Screenplay, and Best Supporting Actor (George Sanders).

4. *The Goddess* (1958)

An ambitious girl seeks fame in Hollywood. Story is based on Marilyn Monroe's life, beautifully acted by Kim Stanley.

5. *The Carpetbaggers* (1964)

Harold Robbins's saga brought to the screen—the biography of a millionaire plane manufacturer played by George Peppard and closely resembling Howard Hughes, who also makes movies and girls on the side. Carroll Baker is a Jean Harlow type.

6. *Valley of the Dolls* (1967)

Patty Duke plays a Judy Garland character in this appalingly bad adaptation of Jacqueline Susann's apallingly bad book.

7. *The Godfather* (1972)

The life of a Mafia patriarch masterfully acted by Marlon Brando; Al Martino plays a Frank Sinatra prototype.

8. *The Last Tycoon* (1976)

Robert DeNiro portrays a great movie producer of the 1930's who is slowly working himself to death. F. Scott Fitzgerald's last novel on which this movie is based, portrays the life of Irving Thalberg.

9. *New York, New York* (1977)

Liza Minnelli gives a frenetic performance as a Doris Day-type character in love with Robert DeNiro, a musician who gives her a bad time.

10. *The Greek Tycoon* (1978)

Anthony Quinn and Jacqueline Bisset play Aristotle Onassis and Jacqueline Kennedy—badly, but on beautiful sets.

8 MOVIES ABOUT ANTI-SEMITISM

1. *The Wandering Jew* (1933)
2. *June Suss* (1934)
3. *The Great Dictator* (1939)
4. *Gentleman's Agreement* (1947)
5. *I Am a Camera* (1955)
6. *The Diary of Anne Frank* (1959)
7. *The Garden of the Finzi-Continis* (1971)
8. *Cabaret* (1972)

10 FAMOUS MOVIE "DEATHS"

1. *Death Takes a Holiday* (1934,1971)
2. *Death in Small Doses* (1951)
3. *Death of a Salesman* (1951)
4. *Death of a Scoundrel* (1956)
5. *Death of a Gunfighter* (1969)
6. *The Death of Me Yet* (1971)
7. *Death in Venice* (1971)
8. *Death Wish* (1974)
9. *Murder by Death* (1976)
10. *Death on the Nile* (1977)

6
SILENT MOVIES

8 HIGHLY PERSONAL STATEMENTS MADE BY THE STARS ABOUT EACH OTHER

1. MARY PICKFORD

"She was the girl every young man wanted to have—as his sister."
Allistair Cooke

2. JANE RUSSELL

"There are two good reasons why men will go to see her."
Howard Hughes

3. IRVING THALBERG

"Wherever Thalberg sits is always the head of the table."
F. L. Collins

4. RUDOLPH VALENTINO

"Here was one who was catnip to women."
H.L. Mencken

5. MARLON BRANDO

"Most of the time he sounds like he has his mouth full of wet toilet paper."
Rex Reed

6. ORSON WELLES

."There but for the grace of God goes God."
Herman Mankiewicz

7. KATHARINE HEPBURN

"You could throw a hat at her and wherever it hit, it would stick."
Robert Hopkins

8. MARY PICKFORD

"It took longer to make one of Mary's contracts than it did to make one of Mary's pictures."
Samuel Goldwyn

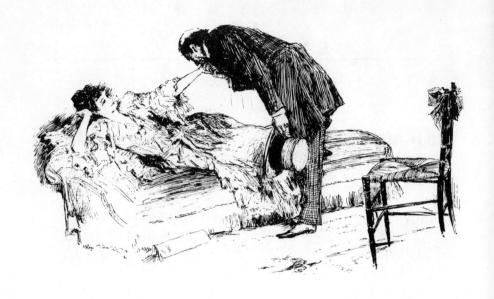

HOLLYWOOD'S FIRST 10 STARS

1. FLORENCE LAWRENCE

She was first known only as the "Biograph Girl," then as the "Imp Girl" when she moved over to the rival company, Carl Laemmle's Imp Company, in 1908. The first movie actors were anonymous, and it was only because the public demanded it that their names eventually had to be released.

2. BRONCHO BILLY ANDERSON

Known throughout the world as "Broncho Billy" the absolute prototype of the heroic, acrobatic, equestrian star, he actually hated riding horses and faked most of his stunts. His career died with the death of two-reelers but by that time he had permanently fixed the pattern of the western movie.

3. MAURICE COSTELLO

A stage Englishman and the first matinee idol, Costello's popularity was partly due to his haggard appearance, which his devoted fans took for a sign of dissipation and therefore of worldly experience.

4. FRANCIS X. BUSHMAN

Bushman is the best remembered of the early matinee

idols. His popularity was so great that once when he appeared in Chicago he caused a full-scale riot.

5. SARAH BERNHARDT

As early as 1900 Sarah Bernhardt, the greatest actress of them all, had filmed the duel scene from *Hamlet* (in which she played the title role) and by 1911 she was making pictures regularly. American audiences first saw her in *Queen Elizabeth* in 1912, a film that even then seemed static and uninspiring.

6. MARY PICKFORD

Film historian Edgar Wagenknecht sums up Mary Pickford's screen image. "She was America's sweetheart, America's darling child, America's problem child, and at times the Madonna. No matter who she played, however, her character had to have sincerity of purpose." She died on May 29, 1979, at eighty-six.

7. CHARLES CHAPLIN

Probably the screen's greatest genius ever, Chaplin remained modest to the end. "Imagine," he once said, "Churchill expressed disappointment because I had not replied to a fan letter he had written me. Think of Churchill even remembering that I had failed to answer him. Me!"

8. RUTH ROLAND

Ruth Roland was the tomboy heroine of countless serials, mostly Westerns. Her popularity waned in the twenties, but by that time she had saved enough money to finance her own movies. The added expense of the talkies, however, put an end to her independent ventures and Miss Roland retreated to grace Hollywood drawing rooms instead.

9. WALLACE REID

The epitome to the clean cut, or, as it was known then, the "Arrow Collar" look, Wallace Reid rose from a bit part in *The Birth of a Nation* (1915) to spectacular stardom as every flapper's dream. He was the ideal young American—virile, aggressive, gay, imaginative, and handsome. No one could then foresee his agonized death from drug addiction ten years later.

10. PAULINE FREDERICK

Pauline Frederick was a universally respected star of screen, stage, and vaudeville for thirty years, possessing classical beauty, magnetism, and dynamic acting genius.

Lillian Gish owed her movie career to brains, beauty, and the genius of D.W. Griffith.

AMERICA'S 10 MOST FAMOUS SILENT MOVIE STARS

1. Charles Chaplin—the supreme acting genius
2. Mary Pickford—America's Sweetheart
3. Rudolph Valentino—The Sheik
4. Clara Bow—The "It" Girl. "It" was then the term for sex appeal.
5. Ramon Novarro—the Latin lover
6. Douglas Fairbanks—the great swashbuckler
7. Lillian Gish—the perennial victim
8. John Barrymore—The Great Profile
9. Theda Bara—The Vamp
10. Gloria Swanson—Paramount's number-one female star

AMERICA'S 10 MOST FAMOUS SILENT FILMS

1. *Intolerance* (1916)
   A D.W. Griffith classic, starring Lillian Gish and Constance Talmadge
2. *Shoulder Arms* (1918)
   with Charles Chaplin
3. *Broken Blossoms* (1919)
   One of D.W. Griffith's most successful films, starring Lillian Gish and Richard Barthelemess
4. *The Sheik* (1921)
   with Rudolph Valentino
5. *The Prisoner of Zenda* (1922)
   with Ramon Novarro and Alice Terry
6. *Greed* (1923)
   This Erich Von Stroheim masterpiece originally ran for eight hours

154

"America's Sweetheart" was really a Canadian—Mary Pickford.

7. *The Ten Commandments* (1923)
   Cecil B. De Mille's first epic

8. *The Gold Rush* (1925)
   The best-loved Charles Chaplin film

9. *The Student Prince* (1927)
   with Norma Shearer and Ramon Novarro

10. *The Understanding Heart* (1927)
    with Joan Crawford

Before he shot to stardom after the tango sequence in The
Four Horsemen of the Apocalypse *(1921), Rudolph Valentino
eked out a living as a gigolo.*

10 INTERESTING FACTS ABOUT SILENT MOVIES

1. Although Thomas Alva Edison discovered the kinetoscope in 1876, he never fully realized its potential. (A kinetoscope was a motion picture device in which the film passed beneath a peephole and was seen by a single viewer.) He did, however, exploit his new invention by showing it in penny arcades and peep shows.

2. The early motion picture companies did not release the names of their actors but labelled them with the companies' names instead—the best known of which was the "Biograph Girl." (Florence Lawrence)

3. "America's Sweetheart" was really a Canadian—Mary Pickford.

4. Rudolph Valentino (1895-1926) was a well-known gigolo in Hollywood before he became a star. He shot to stardom after movie audiences saw the tango sequence in *The Four Horsemen of the Apocalypse* (1921).

5. Charles Chaplin's brother Sidney (1885-1965) was also a silent star. He appeared in many silent two-reelers and several features before retiring when sound came in.

6. Mary Pickford, Charles Chaplin, D.W. Griffith, and Douglas Fairbanks formed the United Artists Corporation in 1919 when the studios they had been working for refused to meet their astronomical salary demands.

7. Samuel Goldwyn's real name was Samuel Goldfish.

8. Because of the many drug and sex scandals of the early years of Hollywood, a code of ethics was set up in 1922. It controlled what happened on the screen and even made the stars sign morality contracts—with debatable degrees of success.

9. Gloria Swanson made her film debut in 1915 in *The Fable of Elvira and Farina and the Meal Ticket.*

10. Filmmaker D.W. Griffith demanded that all his leading ladies have long curly blond hair, delicate hands and feet, big sad eyes, and bee-stung lips. They—notably Lillian Gish, Mary

Pickford, Blanche Sweet, Mae Marsh—all looked more like dolls than women and were meant to represent the helpless heroines of Victorian fiction.

MARY PICKFORD'S 10 MOST FAMOUS FILMS

1. *Rebecca of Sunnybrook Farm* (1917)
2. *Poor Little Rich Girl* (1919)
3. *Daddy Long Legs* (1919)
4. *Pollyanna* (1920)
5. *Tess of the Storm Country* (1922)
6. *Rosita* (1923)
7. *Sparrows* (1926)
8. *My Best Girl* (1927)
9. *Coquette* (1929)
10. *Secrets* (1933)

RUDOLPH VALENTINO'S 10 MOST FAMOUS FILMS

1. *Stolen Moments* (1920)
2. *The Conquering Power* (1921)
3. *The Four Horsemen of the Apocalypse* (1921)
4. *Camille* (1921)
5. *The Sheik* (1921)
6. *Blood and Sand* (1922)
7. *Monsieur Beaucaire* (1924)
8. *The Cobra* (1925)
9. *The Eagle* (1926)
10. *Son of the Sheik* (1926)

CHARLIE CHAPLIN'S 12 FEATURE FILMS

1. *Tillie's Punctured Romance* (1914)
   with Mabel Normand and Marie Dressler
2. *The Kid* (1921)
   with Jackie Coogan and Edna Purviance
3. *A Woman of Paris* (1923)
4. *The Gold Rush* (1923)
5. *The Circus* (1928)
6. *City Lights* (1931)
   with Virginia Cherrill
7. *Modern Times* (1936)
   with Paulette Goddard
8. *The Great Dictator* (1940)
   with Paulette Goddard
9. *Monsieur Verdoux* (1947)
10. *Limelight* (1952)
    with Claire Bloom
11. *A King in New York* (1957)
12. *A Countess from Hong Kong* (1967)
    with Sophia Loren and Marlon Brando

Lon Chaney Jr., son of "The Man of 1,000 Faces," became a star only after he changed his name. He made 150 movies!

7
MONSTERS AND WESTERNS

THE 10 MOST FAMOUS HORROR STARS

1. LON CHANEY SR.

"The Man of a Thousand Faces" was, in his heyday in the silent twenties, a master of pantomime and disguise, often going to incredible pains and painful contortions to achieve the effects he desired. His greatest triumph was as the deformed bellringer, Quasimodo, in *The Hunchback of Notre Dame* (1923).

2. LON CHANEY JR.

The son of Lon Chaney, he became a star only after he changed his name, which was originally Creighton Chaney. After an unsuccessful stint as a songwriter, Lon Chaney Jr. made many superbly realistic horror movies, among them *Wolf Man* in 1941. He died in 1973 of throat cancer—the same disease that felled his father in 1930.

3. LIONEL ATWILL

Lionel Atwill's forte was playing inventors, mad scientists, and terrorists. He terrorized a South Sea island in *Mad Doctor of Market Street* (1942); he waxed corpses in *Mystery of the Wax Museum* (1933). Occasionally he was brilliant—as, for example, the wooden-armed Inspector Krogh in *Son of Frankenstein* (1939).

4. BORIS KARLOFF

Boris Karloff gave dignity, intelligence, and credibility even to the silliest movies, and for more than thirty-five years he held his public's interest, growing ever more photogenic with advancing age. He died in 1969—a great loss to the genre he had so creatively served.

5. VINCENT PRICE

Star of such horror films as *House of Wax* (1953), *The Mad Magician* (1954), *The Pit and the Pendulum* (1961), Vincent Price's most frightening role was as the revengeful doctor who spoke through a metal plug in his throat, played organ music, and killed through the Seven Curses of the Pharaohs. He *was* the *Abominable Dr. Phibes* (1971).

6. BELA LUGOSI

After a long career that included very good *(Dracula)* , mediocre *(Voodoo Man)* , and very bad movies *(Bela Lugosi Meets the Brooklyn Gorilla),* Bela Lugosi died in 1956, having just completed *Bride of the Monster*— a movie of the third category.

7. GEORGE ZUCCO

His films include *The Mummy's Hand* (1940), *The Return of the Ape Man* (1944), and *The Mad Ghoul* (1943), but despite the mediocre material he had to work with, Zucco was a fine actor, having perfected his image of the suave, well-bred Englishman with an evil heart. He died in 1960.

8. JOHN CARRADINE

The top screen villain of the thirties, John Carradine also has such epics as *Voodoo Man* (1944), *The Unearthly* (1957), and *Blood of Dracula* (1957) to his credit. He appeared as recently as 1973 in *The Wax Museum.*

9. MICHAEL GOUGH

Michael Gough, the mad scientist who can turn a chimp into a murderous gorilla, is a very fine English actor who brings dignity and style even to his most mediocre roles.

10. PETER LORRE

As the malevolent killer with the lovable smile, Peter Lorre played the same role over and over again. Hungarian born, he kept enough of his accent to make himself eerily sinister, although in his later movies *(Comedy of Terrors* 1963, and *The Patsy* , 1964) he parodied his screen persona.

10 FAMOUS HORROR ROLES

1. Peter Lorre in *M* (1930)
2. John Barrymore in *Svengali* (1931)
3. Boris Karloff in *The Mummy* (1932)
4. Boris Karloff in *The Ghoul* (1933)
5. Claude Rains in *The Invisible Man* (1933)
6. Harry Hull in *The Werewulf of London* (1935)
7. Gloria Holden in *Dracula's Daughter* (1936)
8. Claude Rains in *The Phantom of the Opera* (1943)
9. Lon Chaney Jr. in *Son of Dracula* (1943)
10. Karl Malden in *The Phantom of the Rue Morgue* (1954)

THE 13 BEST-KNOWN FRANKESTEIN MOVIES

1. *Frankenstein* (1931)
2. *The Bride of Frankenstein* (1935)
3. *The Son of Frankenstein* (1939)
4. *The Ghost of Frankenstein* (1942)
5. *Frankenstein Meets the Wolf Man* (1943)
6. *The House of Frankenstein* (1945)
7. *Abbott and Costello Meet Frankenstein* (1948)
8. *The Curse of Frankenstein* (1956)
9. *Frankenstein's Daughter* (1958)
10. *Frankenstein 1970* (1958)
11. *Evil of Frankenstein* (1959)
12. *I Was a Teenage Frankenstein* (1962)
13. *Dracula vs. Frankenstein* (1971)

Dracula (1931)—probably the best of the Dracula movies.

THE 15 BEST-KNOWN DRACULA MOVIES

1. *Dracula* (1931)
2. *Dracula's Daughter* (1936)
3. *Son of Dracula* (1943)
4. *House of Dracula* (1945)
5. *Horror of Dracula* (1958)
6. *The Brides of Dracula* (1960)
7. *Dracula—Prince of Darkness* (1965)
8. *Billy the Kid vs. Dracula* (1966)
9. *Dracula Has Risen from the Grave* (1968)
10. *Dracula Must Be Destroyed* (1969)
11. *Taste the Blood of Dracula* (1970)
12. *Countess Dracula* (1970)
13. *Scars of Dracula* (1970)
14. *Dracula AD 1972* (1972)
15. *Dracula Is Dead and Well and Living in London* (1973)

10 FAMOUS FEMALE MONSTERS

1. Elsa Lanchester in *Bride of Frankenstein* (1935)
2. Gloria Holden as Marya Zaleska in *Dracula's Daughter* (1936)
3. Simone Simon as Irena Dubrovna in *The Cat People* (1942) and *The Curse of the Cat People* (1944)
4. Gale Sondergaard as *The Spider Woman* (1946)
5. Mari Blanchard as the maniacal murderess in *The She Devil* (1957)
6. Barbara Steele as a sexy sorceress in *Black Sunday* (1960)
7. Coleen Gray as *The Leech Woman* (1960)
8. Ingrid Pitt, the "Queen of Horror," in *The Vampire Lovers* (1971), *The House that Dripped Blood* (1971), *Countess Dracula* (1970)
9. Susan Cabot as *The Wasp Woman*
10. Acquanetta as *The Ape Woman*

THE 10 MOST FAMOUS HOLLYWOOD WESTERNS

1. *The Ox-Bow Incident* (1943)
2. *She Wore a Yellow Ribbon* (1940)
3. *The Gunfighter* (1950)
4. *High Noon* (1952)
5. *Shane* (1953)
6. *Johnny Guitar* (1954)
7. *Bad Day at Black Rock* (1954)
8. *Cat Ballou* (1965)
9. *True Grit* (1969)
10. *Butch Cassidy and the Sundance Kid* (1970)

10 FAMOUS HISTORICAL WESTERN HEROES

1. Billy the Kid
2. Davy Crockett
3. Wild Bill Hickok
4. Jesse James
5. General Custer

6. Wyatt Earp
7. Annie Oakley
8. Sitting Bull
9. Buffalo Bill
10. Doc Holliday

9 FILMS ABOUT BILLY THE KID (WILLIAM BONNEY, 1860-1881)

1. *Billy the Kid* (1930)
2. *Billy the Kid Returns* (1932)
3. *Billy the Kid (1940)*
4. *The Outlaw* (1943)
5. *The Law versus Billy the Kid* (1954)
6. *The Parson and the Outlaw* (1957)
7. *The Left-handed Gun* (1958)
8. *Chisum* (1970)
9. *Dirty Little Billy* (1972)

THE FIRST 6 WESTERN MOVIE STARS

1. TOM MIX (1881-1941)

   Mix made more than four hundred action-packed movies before he was killed in a car crash.

2. WILLIAM SURREY HART (1870-1946)

   The first sympathetic villain, Hart's career petered out in the mid 1920's when realism went out of style.

3. HOOT GIBSON (1892-1962)

   Gibson's long career began with *The Cactus Kid* in 1919 and ended with *The Horse Soldiers* in 1959.

4. GENE AUTRY (1907-

   Autry was the original singing cowboy. Who can forget his guitar and his horse *Champion* , and such classics as *Guns and Saddles* (1949) and *Carolina Moon* (1940)?

5. WILLIAM BOYD (1898-1972)

   Boyd, the beloved Hopalong Cassidy, was particularly popular among children.

6. TEX RITTER (1907-

   Ritter starred in many, many second-rate westerns in the 1930's and 1940's.

10 UNLIKELY WESTERN MOVIE STARS

1. Marlene Dietrich in *Destry Rides Again* (1939)

2. Boris Karloff in *Tap Roots* (1948)

3. Grace Kelly in *High Noon* (1952)

4. Lon Chaney in *High Noon* (1952)

5. Audrey Hepburn in *The Unforgiven* (1960)

6. Jon Voight in *The Hour of the Gun* (1967)

7. Brigitte Bardot in *Shalako* (1968)

8. Jeanne Moreau in *Monte Walsh* (1970)

9. Katharine Ross in *Butch Cassidy and the Sundance Kid* (1970)

10. Shirley MacLaine in *Two Mules for Sister Sara* (1970)

HOLLYWOOD'S 10 GREATEST WESTERN STARS

1. John Wayne
2. Henry Fonda
3. Charles Bronson
4. Clint Eastwood
5. Glenn Ford

6. James Stewart
7. Andy Devine
8. Joel McCrea
9. Burt Lancaster
10. Roy Rogers

8
MUSICALS

10 FAMOUS MALE VOCALISTS AND THEIR MOST POPULAR ROLES

1. Nelson Eddy in *Rose Marie* (1936)
2. Paul Robeson in *Show Boat* (1936)
3. Al Jolson in *The Jolson Story* (1946) (voice only)
4. Gene Kelly in *Singin' in the Rain* (1952)
5. Bing Crosby in *White Christmas* (1954)
6. Frank Sinatra in *Pal Joey* (1957)
7. Maurice Chevalier in *Gigi* (1958)
8. Elvis Presley in *Blue Hawaii* (1961)
9. The Beatles in *Hard Day's Night* (1964)
10. Chris Kristofferson in *A Star Is Born* (1977)

Variety

10 FAMOUS FEMALE VOCALISTS AND THEIR MOST POPULAR ROLES

1. Marlene Dietrich in *The Blue Angel* (1930)
2. Jeanette MacDonald in *San Francisco* (1936)
3. Judy Garland in *The Wizard of Oz* (1939)
4. Ethel Merman in *Call Me Madam* (1953)
5. Doris Day in *Love Me or Leave Me* (1955)
6. Mary Martin in *South Pacific* (1958)

7. Julie Andrews in *The Sound of Music* (1965)

8. Barbra Streisand in *Funny Girl* (1968)

9. Liza Minnelli in *Cabaret* (1972)

10. Diana Ross in *Lady Sings the Blues* (1972)

Variety

10 FAMOUS SONGS SUNG BY STARS IN THE MOVIES

1. "The Way We Were"—Barbra Streisand

2. "Over the Rainbow"—Judy Garland

3. "Lilli Marlene"—Marlene Dietrich

4. "Swanee River"—Al Jolson

5. "White Christmas"—Bing Crosby

6. "My Favorite Things"—Julie Andrews

7. "Singin' in the Rain"—Gene Kelly

8. "I've Grown Accustomed to Her Face"—Rex Harrison

9. "Cabaret"—Liza Minnelli

10. "Laura"—Frank Sinatra

10 OF FRED ASTAIRE'S DANCING PARTNERS

1. Joan Crawford in *Dancing Lady* (1933)

2. Ginger Rogers in *Top Hat* (1935)

3. Eleanor Powell in *Broadway Melody of 1940* (1940)

4. Paulette Goddard in *Second Chorus* (1940)

5. Rita Hayworth in *You Were Never Lovelier* (1942)

6. Judy Garland in *Easter Parade* (1948)

7. Betty Hutton in *Let's Dance* (1950)

170

Joan Crawford starred with Fred Astaire in Dancing Lady *in (1933).*

8. Vera-Ellen in *Three Little Words* (1950)

9. Cyd Charisse in *The Band Wagon* (1953)

10. Leslie Caron in *Daddy Long Legs* (1955)

Fred Astaire and Ginger Rogers created six of Hollywood's most popular dance movies of the thirties.

6 FRED ASTAIRE AND GINGER ROGERS MOVIES

1. *Flying Down to Rio* (1933)
2. *The Gay Divorcée* (1934)
3. *Roberta* (1934)
4. *Follow the Fleet* (1935)
5. *Top Hat* (1935)
6. *Shall We Dance?* (1937)

172

Gene Kelly starred in Singin' in the Rain — *perhaps the greatest Hollywood musical ever made.*

GENE KELLY'S 10 GREATEST MOVIE MUSICALS

1. *For Me and My Gal* (1942)
   with Judy Garland
2. *Cover Girl* (1944)
   with Rita Hayworth

Fred Astaire and Gene Kelly hosted That's Entertainment
Part 2 *in 1976.*

3. *Take Me Out to the Ball Game* (1949)
    with Esther Williams and Betty Garrett

4. *Summer Stock* (1950)
    with Judy Garland

5. *An American in Paris* (1951)
    with Leslie Caron

6. *Singin' in the Rain* (1952)
    with Debbie Reynolds

7. *Brigadoon* (1954)
    with Cyd Charisse

8. *Les Girls* (1957)
    with Kay Kendall

9. *Let's Make Love* (1960)
    with Marilyn Monroe

10. *That's Entertainment, Part 2* (1976)
    MGM musical cavalcade

10 ACTORS WHO HAVE PLAYED COMPOSERS IN THE MOVIES

1. Don Ameche as Steven Foster in *Swanee River* (1939)

2. Victor Mature as Paul Dresser in *My Gal Sal* (1942)

3. Robert Alda as George Gershwin in *Rhapsody in Blue* (1945)

4. Cary Grant as Cole Porter in *Night and Day* (1945)

5. Tom Drake as Richard Rodgers in *Words and Music* (1948)

6. Mickey Rooney as Lorenz Hart in *Words and Music* (1948)

7. Jose Ferrer as Sigmund Romberg in *Deep in My Heart* (1954)

8. Nat King Cole as W.C. Handy in *St. Louis Blues* (1958)

9. Dirk Bogarde as Franz Liszt in *Song without End* (1960)

10. Richard Chamberlain as Peter Tchaikovsky in *The Music Lovers* (1971)

10 MUSICAL BIOGRAPHIES

1. *Swanee River* (1939)—Steven Foster
2. *Dixie* (1943)—Dan Emmett
3. *A Song to Remember* (1945)—Frederic Chopin
4. *Rhapsody in Blue* (1945)—George Gershwin
5. *Night and Day* (1945)—Cole Porter
6. *The Jolson Story* (1946)—Al Jolson
7. *Jolson Sings Again* (1949)—Al Jolson
8. *The Great Caruso* (1951)—Enrico Caruso
9. *Funny Girl* (1968)—Fanny Brice
10. *Funny Lady* (1975)—Fanny Brice

9
TRIVIA

10 OF HOLLYWOOD'S MOST TRIVIAL QUOTATIONS

1. "Let's bring it up to date with some snappy nineteenth-century dialogue."

   Samuel Goldwyn

2. "The only thing I worry about is dying without a cigarette in my mouth."

   Bette Davis, on her seventieth birthday

3. "It may be that Miss Garbo cannot act, but what she does instead is more interesting than any acting I have seen."

   movie critic of the 1930's

4. "The movies are the only place where you can sit in the audience and applaud yourself."

   Will Rogers

5. "What we want is a story that starts with an earthquake and works its way up to a climax."

   Samuel Goldwyn

6. "I like to be introduced as America's foremost actor. It saves the necessity of further effort."

   John Barrymore

7. UNABLE OBTAIN BIDET. SUGGEST HANDSTAND IN SHOWER.

   Billy Wilder in Paris, in reply to his wife's request to get her a bidet for their Hollywood home

8. "When I cry, do you want the tears to run all the way, or shall I stop halfway down?"

   Margaret O'Brien

9. "I have eyes like those of a dead pig."

   Marlon Brando

"I like to be introduced as America's foremost actor."
John Barrymore

10. "I may not be a great actress but I've become the greatest at screen orgasms. Ten seconds of heavy breathing, roll your head from side to side, simulate a slight asthma attack, and die a little."
Candice Bergen

10 MOVIE WARDROBES THAT CREATED FADS OR FASHIONS

1. Clark Gable's lack of an undershirt in *It Happened One Night* (1934)

2. Fred Astaire's cravat in *Top Hat* (1935)

3. Shirley Temple's curls in *Rebecca of Sunnybrook Farm* (1938)

4. Bing Crosby's pipe in *Going My Way* (1944)

5. Marlon Brando's T-shirt in *A Streetcar Named Desire* (1951)

6. James Dean's windbreaker in *Rebel without a Cause* (1955)

7. Elvis Presley's tight pants in *Jailhouse Rock* (1957)

8. Elizabeth Taylor's white chiffon cocktail dress in *Cat on a Hot Tin Roof* (1958)

9. Audrey Hepburn's dark glasses in *Two for the Road* (1967)

10. John Travolta's white disco suit in *Saturday Night Fever* (1977)

Clark Gable's lack of an undershirt in It Happened One Night *(1934) created one of Hollywood's most surprising fads.*

10 WELL-KNOWN FEMALE MOVIE DIRECTORS

1. Elaine May— *A New Leaf* (1972), *The Heartbreak Kid* (1972)

2. Kirsten Stenback— *The Dreamers* (1966), *Do You Believe in Witches?*, *The Lenin Gang* (1972)

3. Vera Chytilova— *The Ceiling* (1960), *Something Different* (1963), *Daisies* (1965), *Le Fruit du Paradis* (1971)

4. Kate Millett— *Three Lives* (1970)

5. Barbara Loden— *Wanda* (1970)

6. Nelly Kaplan— *La Fiancée du Pirate* (Dirty Mary) (1969), *Papa les Petits Bateaux* (1971)

7. Muriel Box— *Rattle of a Simple Man* (1964), *Subway in the Sky* (1958), *The Passionate Stranger* (1956), *To Dorothy a Son* (1954), *Happy Family* (1952)

8. Mai Zetterling— *Night Games* (1965), *Loving Couples* (1964), *The War Game* (1963)

9. Ida Lupino— *The Hitch Hiker* (1953), *The Trouble with Angels* (1966), *Hard, Fast, and Beautiful* (1951)

10. Lena Weirtmuller— *The Seduction of Mimi* (1972), *Swept Away* (1974), and *Seven Beauties* (1976) are her most successful films.

10 INTERESTING MOVIE FACTS

1. Elizabeth Taylor disguised herself as a boy in *National Velvet* (1944). She was twelve years old.

2. Gene Kelly's most unusual dancing partner was a cartoon mouse in *Anchors Aweigh* (1945).

3. A film that first starred Rudolph Valentino was remade twenty-two years later starring Bob Hope — *Monsieur Beaucaire* (1946).

4. Adolph Zukor, the president of Paramount Pictures, was the film industry's first centenarian. He was born in 1873 and died in 1976.

5. Alec Guinness played no less than eight parts in *Kind Hearts and Coronets* (1949).

6. The romantic singing team of Jeanette MacDonald and Nelson Eddy were known, less than affectionately, as "The Iron Butterfly" and "The Singing Capon."

7. One of the most extravagantly romantic lines ever said in the movies was: "Waiter, you see that moon? I want to see that moon in the champagne . . . " The film was *Trouble in Paradise* (1932); the speaker, Herbert Marshall.

When Monsieur Beaucaire, *starring Rudolph Valentino, was remade twenty-two years later in 1946, Bob Hope was the surprising choice for the lead.*

181

8. W.C. Fields' most unusual role was that of Humpty Dumpty in the 1933 version of *Alice in Wonderland.*

9. The film, *Krakatoa: East of Java* (1969) has an incorrect title. Krakatoa is actually *west* of Java.

10. Edward G. Robinson's real name was Emmanuel Goldenberg.

10 INGENIOUS HOLLYWOOD PUBLICITY LINES

1. "He treated her rough—and she loved it!"
   Red Dust (1932)

2. "She knows all about love potions and lovely motions!"
   I Married a Witch (1942)

3. "How'd you like to tussle with Russell?"
   The Outlaw (1943)

4. "The minx in mink with a yen for men!"
   Lady in the Dark (1944)

5. "The sum total of all human emotion!"
   Leave Her to Heaven (1945)

6. "She's got the biggest six-shooters in the West!"
   The Beautiful Blonde from Bashful Bend (1949)

7. "A thousand thrills . . . and Hayley Mills!"
   In Search of the Castaways (1962)

8. "They're young . . . they're in love . . . and they kill people."
   Bonnie and Clyde (1967)

9. "Love means never having to say you're sorry."
   Love Story (1970)

10. "The story of a homosexual who married a nymphomaniac."
    The Music Lovers (1971)

10 UNUSUAL MOVIE PLOTS

1. A caterpillar dances to "Yes, Sir, That's My Baby," in *Once Upon a Time* (1944).
2. God speaks on the radio in *The Next Voice You Hear* (1950).
3. A cat becomes the owner of a baseball team in *Rhubarb* (1950).
4. An atomic cloud makes a man smaller and smaller until he becomes invisible in *The Incredible Shrinking Man* (1957).
5. A cat avenges his mistress's murder in *Shadow of the Cat* (1962).
6. Birds follow and attack a girl in an isolated California community in *The Birds* (1963).
7. A shy man turns into a happy dolphin in *The Incredible Mr. Limpet* (1964).
8. A girl has the strange power to change into a snake in *The Reptile* (1966).
9. A football player comes back to life as a multi-millionaire who has been murdered by his wife in *Heaven Can Wait* (1978).
10. A twelve-year-old New Orleans prostitute marries an older photographer in *Pretty Baby* (1978).

10 MOVIES IN WHICH WELL-KNOWN PERSONALITIES APPEARED AS THEMSELVES

1. *The Great Ziegfeld* (1936)—Fanny Brice
2. *Wake Up and Live* (1937)—Walter Winchell
3. *They Shall Have Music* (1939)—Jascha Heifetz
4. *Pride of the Yankees* (1942)—Babe Ruth
5. *Sunset Boulevard* (1950)—Cecil B. DeMille
6. *Pat and Mike* (1952)—Don Budge
7. *The Greatest Show on Earth* (1952)—John Ringling North

Joan Fontaine and Laurence Olivier starred in the brilliant 1940 romance Rebecca, *adapted from Daphne du Maurier's famous novel.*

8. *The Blue Gardenia* (1953)—Nat "King" Cole

9. *The Glenn Miller Story* (1954)—Gene Krupa

10. *High Society* (1955)—Louis Armstrong

10 FAMOUS MOVIES THAT WERE ORIGINALLY NOVELS

1. *The Grapes of Wrath* (1940) by John Steinbeck

2. *Rebecca* (1940) by Daphne du Maurier

3. *For Whom the Bell Tolls* (1943) by Ernest Hemingway

4. *Oliver Twist* (1948) by Charles Dickens

5. *The Great Gatsby* (1949 and 1974) by F. Scott Fitzgerald

6. *Breakfast at Tiffany's* (1961) by Truman Capote

7. *Tom Jones* (1963) by Henry Fielding

8. *The Group* (1966) by Mary McCarthy

9. *Far from the Madding Crowd* (1967) by Thomas Hardy

10. *Death in Venice* (1971) by Thomas Mann

Laurence Olivier played Hamlet *(1948) in an Academy Award-winning role of the play by Shakespeare.*

10 FAMOUS MOVIES THAT WERE ORIGINALLY PLAYS

1. *Pygmalion* (1978) by George Bernard Shaw
2. *Hamlet* (1948) by Willian Shakespeare
3. *The Glass Menagerie* (1950) by Tennessee Williams
4. *Death of a Salesman* (1952) by Arthur Miller
5. *Come Back, Little Sheba* (1952) by William Inge
6. *Cat on a Hot Tin Roof* (1958) by Tennessee Williams
7. *The Entertainer* (1960) by John Osborne
8. *Long Day's Journey into Night* (1962) by Eugene O'Neill
9. *Who's Afraid of Virginia Woolf* (1966) by Edward Albee
10. *Entertaining Mr. Sloane* (1970) by Joe Orton

10 WOMEN'S NAMES THAT HAVE BEEN MOVIE TITLES

1. *Emma* (1932) played by Marie Dressler
2. *Heidi* (1937) played by Shirley Temple
3. *Rebecca* (1940) played by Joan Fontaine
4. *Laura* (1944) played by Gene Tierney
5. *Anna* (1951) played by Silvana Mangano
6. *Gigi* (1958) played by Leslie Caron
7. *Gidget* (1959) played by Sandra Dee
8. *Ada* (1961) played by Susan Hayworth
9. *Fanny* (1961) played by Leslie Caron
10. *Gypsy* (1962) played by Natalie Wood

10 ACTORS WHO PLAYED SECOND FIDDLE TO GRETA GARBO

1. Charles Bickford in *Anna Christie* (1930)
2. Lionel Barrymore in *Mata Hari* (1931)
3. Clark Gable in *Susan Lenox: Her Fall and Rise* (1931)
4. Ramon Novarro in *Mata Hari* (1931)
5. John Barrymore in *Grand Hotel* (1932)
6. John Gilbert in *Queen Christina* (1933)
7. Fredric March in *Anna Karenina* (1935)
8. Robert Taylor in *Camille* (1936)
9. Charles Boyer in *Marie Walewska* (1937)
10. Melvyn Douglas in *Two-Faced Woman* (1941) and *Ninotchka* (1939)

Clark Gable played second fiddle to Greta Garbo in 1931.

10 FAMOUS "DRINKING" MOVIES

1. *The Fatal Glass of Beer* (1933)
    with W.C. Fields

2. *The Bitter Tea of General Yen* (1933)
    with Barbara Stanwyck

3. *Champagne Waltz* (1937)
    with Fred MacMurray

4. *Duck Soup* (1933)
    with the Marx Brothers—Groucho, Harpo, Chico, Zeppo

5. *Champagne for Caesar* (1950)
    with Celeste Holm, Ronald Coleman, Vincent Price

6. *Tea for Two* (1950)
    with Doris Day and Gordon MacRae

7. *Tea and Sympathy* (1956)
    with Deborah Kerr and John Kerr

8. *Days of Wine and Roses* (1962)
    with Jack Lemmon and Lee Remick

9. *Under Milk Wood* (1973)
    with Richard Burton

10. *Coffee, Tea, or Me?* (1973)
    Karen Valentine and Louise Lasser

10 FAMOUS "FOOD" MOVIES

1. *Our Daily Bread* (1922)
   with Greta Garbo
2. *The Egg and I* (1947)
   with Claudette Colbert
3. *Wild Strawberries* (1957)
   An Ingmar Bergman film, with Bibi Andersson
4. *Please Don't Eat the Daisies* (1960)
   with Doris Day
5. *The Pumpkin Eater* (1964)
   with Anne Bancroft and Peter Finch
6. *The Fortune Cookie* (1966)
   with Jack Lemmon
7. *Guess Who's Coming to Dinner?* (1967)
   with Katharine Hepburn and Spencer Tracy
8. *Candy* (1968)
   with Marlon Brando and Richard Burton
9. *Bananas* (1971)
   with Woody Allen
10. *Prime Cut* (1972)
    with Lee Marvin

10 MOVIE STARS WHO HAVE PLAYED THE DEVIL

1. Walter Huston in *All that Money Can Buy* (1941)
2. Laird Cregar in *Heaven Can Wait* (1943)
3. Claude Rains in *Angel on My Shoulder* (1946)
4. Stanley Holloway in *Meet Mr. Lucifer* (1953)
5. Vincent Price in *The Story of Mankind* (1957)
6. Ray Walston in *Damn Yankees* (1958)
7. Adolphe Menjou in *The Sorrows of Satan*
8. Allan Mowbray in *The Devil with Hitler*
9. Rex Ingram in *Cabin in the Sky*
10. Ralph Richardson in *Tales from the Crypt* (1972)

10 FAMOUS SCREEN SPIES

1. Nicholas Whistler in *Hot Enough for June* (1964), played by Dirk Bogarde.
2. James Bond in *Goldfinger* (1964), played by Sean Connery.
3. Illya Kuyakin in *The Spy with My Face* (1965), played by David McCallum.
4. Boysie Oakes in *The Liquidator* (1965), played by Rod Taylor.
5. James Bond in *Casino Royale* (1966), played by Ursula Andress.
6. Willie Garvin in *Modesty Blaise* (1966), played by Terence Stamp.
7. Dr. Jason Love in *Where the Spies Are* (1966), played by David Niven.
8. Harry Palmer in *The Billion Dollar Brain* (1967), played by Michael Caine.
9. Derek Flint in *In Like Flint* (1967), played by James Coburn.
10. Matt Helm in *The Wrecking Crew* (1968), played by Dean Martin.

10 COLORFULLY TITLED MOVIES

1. *Blue Angel* (1930)
2. *How Green Was My Valley* (1941)
3. *Forever Amber* (1947)
4. *Yellow Sky* (1948)
5. *Red Hot and Blue* (1949)
6. *Red Planet Mars* (1952)
7. *Black Widow* (1954)
8. *Green Fire* (1954)
9. *White Christmas* (1954)
10. *Blue Water White Death* (1971)

10 FAMOUS MOVIE "NAMES"

1. *Gilda* (1946)
   with Rita Hayworth and Glenn Ford
2. *Anna Karenina* (1948)
   with Vivien Leigh
3. *Anastasia* (1956)
   with Ingrid Bergman and Yul Brynner
4. *Tom Jones* (1963)
   with Albert Finney and Susannah York
5. *Mary Poppins* (1964)
   with Julie Andrews
6. *Bonnie and Clyde* (1967)
   with Warren Beatty and Faye Dunaway
7. *Bob and Carol and Ted and Alice* (1969)
   with Natalie Wood and Dyan Cannon
8. *Bobby Deerfield* (1977)
   with Al Pacino and Marthe Keller

The incomparable Rita Hayworth was never sexier than in Gilda (1946), when she sang "Put the Blame on Mame."

9. *Annie Hall* (1977)
   with Diane Keaton and Woody Allen
10. *Julia* (1977)
    with Jane Fonda and Vanessa Redgrave

10 FAMOUS HOLLYWOOD REMAKES

1. *The Front Page* (1931) with Adolphe Menjou, Pat O'Brien, Maurice Black

   His Girl Friday (1940) with Cary Grant, Rosalind Russell, Ralph Bellamy

   The Front Page (1974) with Walter Matthau, Jack Lemmon

2. *Sadie Thompson* (1928) with Gloria Swanson, Lionel Barrymore

   Rain (1932) with Joan Crawford, Walter Huston

   Miss Sadie Thompson (1954) with Rita Hayworth, Jose Ferrer

3. *Of Human Bondage* (1934) with Bette Davis, Leslie Howard

   Of Human Bondage (1946) with Eleanor Parker, Paul Henreid

   Of Human Bondage (1964) with Kim Novak, Laurence Harvey

4. *Cleopatra* (1917) with Theda Bara

   Cleopatra (1934) with Claudette Colbert

   Cleopatra (1963) with Elizabeth Taylor

5. *Satan Met a Lady* (1936) with Warren Williams, Marie Wilson

   The Maltese Falcon (1941) with Humphrey Bogart, Lee Patrick

   The Black Bird (1976) with George Segal, Lee Patrick

6. *Ben Hur* (1925) with Ramon Novarro

   Ben Hur (1959) with Charlton Heston

Billy Wilder directs Walter Matthau in The Front Page *(1974).*

7. *Bringing Up Baby* (1938) with Cary Grant, Katharine Hepburn

   What's Up Doc (1972) with Ryan O'Neal, Barbra Streisand

8. *Lost Horizon* (1937) with Ronald Colman

   Lost Horizon (1973) with Peter Finch, Michael York

9. *The Great Gatsby* (1926) with Neil Hamilton, Lois Wilson, and Warner Baxter

194

The Front Page *of 1974 (above) was an enormous success even though it had been filmed before—in 1940, and, before that, in 1931.*

The Great Gatsby (1949) with Alan Ladd, Betty Field, Barry Sullivan

The Great Gatsby (1974) with Robert Redford, Mia Farrow, Bruce Dern

10. *It Happened One Night* (1934) with Claudette Colbert, Clark Gable

You Can't Run Away from It (1956) with June Allyson, Jack Lemmon

The original Great Gatsby *(1926) starred Neil Hamilton, Lois Wilson, and Warner Baxter.*

10 MORE FAMOUS HOLLYWOOD REMAKES

1. *The Wagons Roll at Night* (1941) from *Kid Galahad* (1937)
2. *Singapore Woman* (1941) from *Dangerous* (1935)
3. *Escape in the Desert* (1945) from *Petrified Forest* (1936)
4. *One Sunday Afternoon* (1948) from *The Strawberry Blonde* (1941)
5. *Barricade* (1950) from *The Sea Wolf* (1941)
6. *Painting the Clouds with Sunshine* (1951) from *The Gold Diggers of 1933, 1935,* and *1937*
7. *Young at Heart* (1955) from *Four Daughters* (1938)
8. *House of Women* (1962) from *Caged* (1950)
9. *Heaven Can Wait* (1978) from *Here Comes Mr. Jordan* (1941)
10. *The Champ* (1979) from *The Champ* (1931) and *The Clown* (1953)

10 COMEDIES THAT WERE FILMED AGAIN UNDER A DIFFERENT TITLE

1. *Swing High, Swing Low* (1937) became *When My Baby Smiles at Me* (1948).
2. *Lady for a Day* (1933) became *Pocketful of Miracles* (1961).
3. *Midnight* (1939) became *Masquerade in Mexico* (1945).
4. *Libeled Lady* (1936) became *Easy to Wed* (1946).
5. *Bachelor Mother* (1939) became *Bundle of Joy* (1956).
6. *It Started with Eve* (1941) became *I'd Rather Be Rich* (1964).
7. *Tom, Dick, and Harry* (1941) became *The Girl Most Likely* (1957).
8. *Nothing Sacred* (1937) became *Living It Up* (1954).
9. *It Happened One Night* (1934) became *You Can't Run Away from It* (1956).
10. *The Major and The Minor* (1942) became *You're Never Too Young* (1955).

10 MORE COMEDIES THAT WERE FILMED AGAIN UNDER A DIFFERENT TITLE

1. *The More the Merrier* (1943) became *Walk, Don't Run* (1966).
2. *Too Many Husbands* (1940) became *Three for the Show* (1955).
3. *Mad About Music* (1938) became *The Joy Tiger* (1956). (1956).

4. *Brother Rat* (1938) became *About Face* (1952).

5. *Ninotchka* (1939) became *Silk Stockings* (1957).

6. *The Philadelphia Story* (1940) became *High Society* (1956).

7. *True Confession* (1937) became *Cross My Heart* (1949).

8. *My Favorite Wife* (1940) became *Move Over, Darling* (1963).

9. *The Shop around the Corner* (1940) became *In the Good Old Summertime* (1949).

10. *Love Is News* (1937) became *That Wonderful Urge* (1948).

10 ENGLISH-SPEAKING REMAKES OF FOREIGN FILMS

1. *Algiers* (1938) from the French *Pepé le Moko* and *Casbah*

2. *Midnight Episode* (1939) from the French *Monsieur le Souris*

3. *The Unfinished Dance* (1947) from the French *Ballerina*

4. *The Long Night* (1947) from the French *Le Jour se Leve*

5. *The Thirteenth Letter* (1951) from the French *Le Corbeau*

6. *Human Desire* (1954) from the French *La Bête Humaine*

7. *The Magnificent Seven* (1960) from the Japanese *Seven Samurai*

8. *The Outrage* (1964) from the Japanese *Rashomon*

9. *A Fistful of Dollars* (1966) from the Japanese *Yojimbo*
10. *Cop Out* (1968) from the French *Les Inconnus dans la Maison*

10 FAMOUS NEW YORK MOVIES

1. *Broadway Melody of 1938*
2. *Babes on Broadway* (1941)
3. *Tales of Manhattan* (1942)
4. *East Side, West Side* (1949)
5. *The Barclays of Broadway* (1949)
6. *The Belle of New York* (1952)
7. *New York Confidential* (1955)
8. *A King in New York* (1957)
9. *New York, New York* (1977)
10. *Manhattan* (1979)

10 FAMOUS "HOUSE" FILMS

1. *House of Dracula* (1945)
2. *The House on 92nd Street* (1945)
3. *House of Strangers* (1949)
4. *Doctor in the House* (1953)
5. *House of Wax* (1953)
6. *House of Bamboo* (1955)
7. *House on Haunted Hill* (1958)
8. *The House of the Seven Hawks* (1959)
9. *House of Cards* (1969)
10. *The House that Dripped Blood* (1971)

"Certainly, most movie executives were making love to star-lets. But then, so were most of us actors."
Richard Burton

200

10
FLESH AND FANTASY

10 GREAT QUOTATIONS ON SEX

1. "Certainly, most movie executives were making love to starlets. But then, so were most of us actors."
   Richard Burton

2. "There is sex after death. It's just that you won't be able to feel it."
   Lily Tomlin

3. "Sex appeal is fifty percent what you've got and fifty percent what people think you've got."
   Sophia Loren

4. "I've been around so long, I knew Doris Day before she was a virgin."
   Groucho Marx

5. "There is no suspense like the suspense of delayed coition."
   D.W. Griffith

6. "Is that you're sword, or are you just pleased to see me?"
   Mae West

7. "I'm not a real movie star. I still have the same wife I started out with nearly twenty-eight years ago."
   Will Rogers

8. "I'm as pure as the driven slush."
   Tallulah Bankhead

9. "People think I have a sexy walk. Hell, I'm just trying to hold my gut in."
   Robert Mitchum

10. "They are doing things on the screen now that I wouldn't do in bed—if I could."
    Bob Hope

"People think I have an interesting walk. Hell, I'm just trying to hold my gut in."
Robert Mitchum

10 FAMOUS FASHIONS CREATED BY MOVIE STARS

1. The 1930's love affair with platinum blonde hair was started by Jean Harlow. Her white hair was so much a part of her image that after she died rumor had it that her untimely death had been the result of brain damage from peroxide poisoning.

2. There was hardly a man anywhere who did not copy Rudolph Valentino's brilliantined look in the late twenties. It was kept before the public for years after Valentino's death by Fred Astaire, Robert Montgomery, and other screen sophisticates.

3. Ingrid Bergman started a new, more natural look when she appeared with her eyebrows unplucked in *Intermezzo* (1939). Her first English-speaking film, *Intermezzo* is still one of the best love stories ever filmed.

4. Gina Lollobrigida's poodle cut in *Trapeze* (1956) was widely copied, as teen-aged girls stampeded to get rid of their pony tails and their long bobs in an effort to look as much like Gina Lollobrigida as possible.

5. In the late fifties when Elizabeth Taylor started to line her eyes in black and wear pearlized lipstick, the feminine world followed suit.

6. Audrey Hepburn created a new look with her gamine cut, pedal pushers, and ballet slippers in her 1954 hit *Sabrina*.

7. Marilyn Monroe's sexy look—tight black dress, white gloves, platinum blonde hair, and facial mole—was widely copied with various degrees of success in the late fifties.

8. Barbra Streisand's Afro in *A Star Is Born* (1976) became the rage among Americans of both sexes. A style that suited few of its owners, it was, fortunately, shortlived.

9. In *Network* (1976) Faye Dunaway wore her simple silk shirts and well-cut pants and skirts so well, the look became a uniform among women executives of the late seventies.

10. Diane Keaton's baggy pants, man's jacket, shirt, and tie in *Annie Hall* (1977) appeared on young girls all over the world shortly after the movie's release. It was not a flattering fashion.

Jean Harlow started America's love affair with platinum blonde hair in the 1930's.

Ingrid Bergman started a new, more natural look when she appeared with unplucked eyebrows in Intermezzo *(1939).*

THE 10 MOST UNUSUAL ROMANTIC MEETINGS IN THE MOVIES

1. Bette Davis and Paul Henried in *Now, Voyager* (1942)

    They meet on board ship, where each is trying to escape an unhappy past.

2. Trevor Howard and Celia Johnson in *Brief Encounter* (1946)

    A cinder falls in her eye while waiting on a railway station platform. He comes up to her and says, "Can I help? I'm a doctor."

3. Marilyn Monroe and Tom Ewell in *The Seven Year Itch* (1955)

    A tomato plant from her balcony almost falls on top of him.

4. Sean Connery and Ursula Andress in *Dr. No* (1962)

   She comes out of the sea almost naked except for a knife at her waist.

5. Audrey Hepburn and Cary Grant in *Charade* (1963)

   They meet at a ski resort in the Alps when he returns her friend's little boy, who has shot him in the face with a water pistol.

6. Rex Harrison and Elizabeth Taylor in *Cleopatra* (1963)

   She is sent to him as a gift from Caesar concealed in a carpet and tumbles out of it on to the floor as the carpet is unrolled.

7. Julie Andrews and Christopher Plummer in *The Sound of Music* (1965)

   She is sent from a convent, where she is a novice, to look after his children.

8. Anouk Aimée and Jean-Louis Trintignant in *A Man and a Woman* (1966)

   Both are widowed and meet while visiting their children at a boarding school.

9. Jane Fonda and Michael Sarrazin in *They Shoot Horses Don't They?* (1969)

   They accidentally become dance partners in a dance marathon of the thirties, when her partner walks out on her at the last minute.

10. Ryan O'Neal and Ali MacGraw in *Love Story* (1971)

    They fight over a book he has come to borrow from the Radcliffe library where she works.

10 GREAT QUOTES FROM THE MOVIES THAT YOU'LL HEAR USED IN EVERYDAY LIFE

1. "Shut up and deal." *The Apartment* (1960)
2. "Hello, gorgeous." *Funny Girl* (1968)
3. "Do me a favor. Drop dead." *Born Yesterday* (1950)
4. "It's straight down the tube for both of us." *Double Indemnity* (1944)
5. "They can't wipe us out. We'll go on forever. We're the people." *How Green Was My Valley* (1941)
6. "The bottom is loaded with nice people. Only cream and bastards rise." *Harper* (1966)
7. "My cup runneth over." *A Tree Grows in Brooklyn* (1948)
8. "The only thing missing is the bloodhounds snapping at her rear end." *All About Eve* (1950)
9. "Madness . . . madness!" *The Bridge on the River Kwai* (1957)
10. "I'll live to see all of you hang." *Mutiny on the Bounty* (1935)

10 FAMOUS MOVIE TRIANGLES

1. Fredric March, Greta Garbo, and Basil Rathbone in *Anna Karenina* (1935)
2. William Holden, Audrey Hepburn, and Humphrey Bogart in *Sabrina* (1954)
3. Bing Crosby, Grace Kelly, and Frank Sinatra in *High Society* (1956)
4. Dirk Bogarde, Sarah Miles, and James Fox in *The Servant* (1963)
5. Richard Burton, Deborah Kerr, and Ava Gardner in *The Night of the Iguana* (1964)

Grace Kelly created one of Hollywood's famous love triangles with Bing Crosby and Frank Sinatra in High Society *(1956).*

6. Anne Bancroft, Peter Finch, and Maggie Smith in *The Pumpkin Eater* (1964)

7. Jean Simmons, Laurence Harvey, and Honor Blackman in *Life at the Top* (1965)

8. Geraldine Chaplin, Omar Sharif, and Julie Christie in *Dr. Zhivago* (1965)

9. Beryl Reid, Susannah York, and Coral Browne in *The Killing of Sister George* (1968)

10. Jack Nicholson, Candice Bergen, and Arthur Garfunkel in *Carnal Knowledge* (1971)

208

Greta Garbo starred in Anna Karenina *(1935), and created another Hollywood triangle.*

10 MOVIES RICHARD BURTON AND ELIZABETH TAYLOR HAVE MADE TOGETHER (SO FAR)

1. *Cleopatra* (1962)
2. *The VIP's* (1963)
3. *The Sandpiper* (1965)
4. *Who's Afraid of Virginia Wolf?* (1966)
5. *The Comedians* (1967)

Richard Burton and Elizabeth Taylor have made ten movies together—so far!

6. *The Taming of the Shrew* (1967)
7. *Dr. Faustus* (1967)
8. *Boom* (1968)
9. *Under Milk Wood* (1971)
10. *Hammersmith Is Out* (1972)

210

10 FAMOUS MOVIE STARS WHO HAVE PLAYED PROSTITUTES

1. Bette Davis in *Of Human Bondage* (1934)
2. Vivien Leigh in *Waterloo Bridge* (1940)
3. Rita Hayworth in *Miss Sadie Thompson* (1956)
4. Elizabeth Taylor in *Butterfield 8* (1960)
5. Melina Mercouri in *Never on Sunday* (1960)
6. Shirley MacLaine in *Irma la Douce* (1963)
7. Catherine Deneuve in *Belle de Jour* (1966)
8. Sophia Loren in *Lady L* (1966)
9. Jane Fonda in *Klute* (1971)
10. Simone Signoret in *Madame Rosa* (1978)

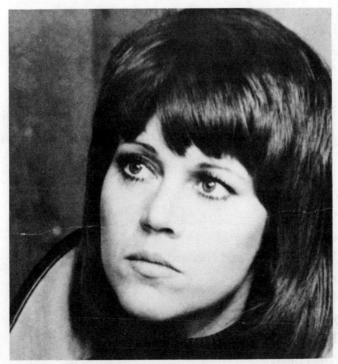

Jane Fonda played a prostitute in Klute *(1971) and won an Oscar for her trouble.*

8 FAMOUS SCREEN "AFFAIRS"

1. *Affair in Trinidad* (1952)
     with Rita Hayworth and Glenn Ford
2. *Affair in Monte Carlo* (1953)
     with Merle Oberon and Richard Todd
3. *Affair with a Stranger* (1953)
     with Victor Mature and Jean Simmons
4. *The End of the Affair* (1955)
     with Deborah Kerr and Van Johnson
5. *Affair in Reno* (1957)
     with John Lund and Doris Singleton
6. *An Affair to Remember* (1957)
     with Cary Grant and Deborah Kerr
7. *Affair in Havana* (1957)
     with Raymond Burr and John Cassavetes
8. *The Affair* (1973)
     with Natalie Wood and Robert Wagner

10 FAMOUS MOVIE "KISSES"

1. *The Kiss* (1929)
     with Greta Garbo
2. *Kiss of Death* (1947)
     with Victor Mature and Richard Widmark
3. *A Kiss in the Dark* (1949)
     with David Niven and Jane Wyman
4. *That Midnight Kiss* (1949)
     with Kathryn Grayson and Mario Lanza
5. *Kiss Me Kate* (1953)
     with Kathryn Grayson and Howard Keel

212

6. *Kiss Me Deadly* (1955)
    with Cloris Leachman and Ralph Meeker
7. *A Kiss Before Dying* (1956)
    with Joanne Woodward and Robert Wagner
8. *Kiss Them for Me* (1957)
    with Cary Grant and Jayne Mansfield
9. *Kiss Me, Stupid* (1964)
    with Dean Martin and Kim Novak
10. *Kiss of Tarantula* (1972)
    with Suzanne Ling

10 FAMOUS MOVIE "CONFESSIONS"

1. *Confession* (1937)
2. *Confessions of a Nazi Spy* (1939)
3. *Confessions of a Boston Blackie* (1941)
4. *I Confess* (1953)
5. *The Confessions of Felix Krull* (1958)
6. *Confessions of an Opium Eater* (1962)
7. *The Confession* (1970)
8. *Confessions of a Police Captain* (1971)
9. *The Confessions of Tom Harris* (1972)
10. *Confessions of a Window Cleaner* (1974)

10 FAMOUS MOVIE "LOVES"

1. *Love* (1927)
    with Greta Garbo and John Gilbert
2. *Love Is a Many Splendored Thing* (1955)
    with Jennifer Jones and William Holden

3. *Love Me Tender* (1956)
   with Elvis Presley

4. *Love in the Afternoon* (1957)
   with Gary Cooper and Audrey Hepburn

5. *Let's Make Love* (1960)
   with Marilyn Monroe

6. *From Russia with Love* (1964)
   with Sean Connery

7. *Love Story* (1970)
   with Ali MacGraw and Ryan O'Neal

8. *Love and Pain (and the Whole Damned Thing)* (1972)
   with Maggie Smith and Timothy Bottoms

9. *Love and Death* (1975)
   with Woody Allen and Diane Keaton

10. *I Love You, I Love You Not* (1979)
    with Jacqueline Bissett

10 FAMOUS "NAKED" MOVIES

1. *The Naked City* (1948)

2. *The Naked Spur* (1953)

3. *The Naked Jungle* (1954)

4. *Naked Alibi* (1954)

5. *The Naked Hills* (1956)

6. *Naked Paradise* (1957)

7. *Naked in the Sun* (1957

8. *The Naked and the Dead* (1958)

9. *The Naked Maja* (1959)

10. *The Naked Runner* (1967)

10 GREAT MOVIE SWASHBUCKLERS

1. Rudolph Valentino in *The Sheik* (1921)
2. J. Warren Kerrigan in *Captain Blood* (1924)
3. Douglas Fairbanks Sr. in *The Black Pirate* (1926)
4. Errol Flynn in *Captain Blood* (1935)
5. Errol Flynn in *The Sea Hawk* (1940)
6. Tyrone Power in *Captain from Castille* (1947)
7. Louis Heyward in *The Fortunes of Captain Blood* (1950)
8. Robert Taylor in *Ivanhoe* (1952)
9. Burt Lancaster in *The Crimson Pirate* (1952)
10. Sean Flynn (son of Errol Flynn) in *Son of Captain Blood* (1962)

10 WELL-KNOWN ERROL FLYNN MOVIES

1. *The Dawn Patrol* (1938)
2. *Virginia City* (1940)
3. *Dive Bomber* (1941)
4. *Edge of Darkness* (1943)
5. *San Antonio* (1945)
6. *Never Say Good-bye* (1946)
7. *Cry Wolf* (1947)
8. *Kim* (1950)
9. *Against All Flags* (1952)
10. *Too Much Too Soon* (1958)

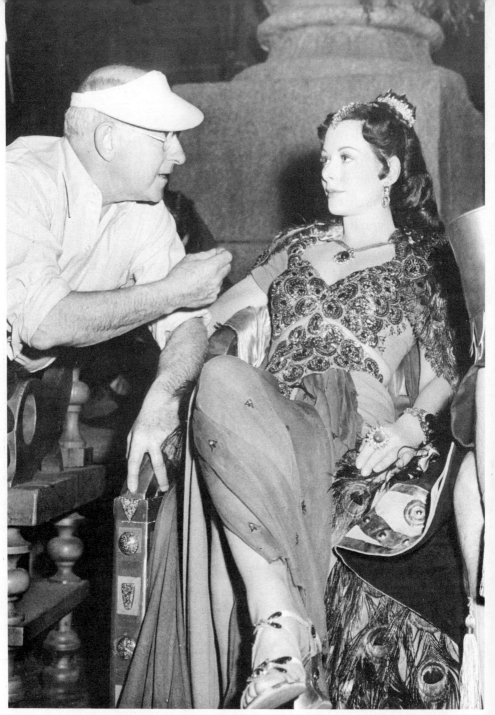

"To be a star is to own the world and all the people in it. After a taste of stardom, everything else is poverty."
Hedy Lamarr

10 QUOTATIONS ABOUT THE HOLLYWOOD STAR SYSTEM

1. "Show me an actress who isn't a personality and I'll show you a woman who isn't a star."

   Katharine Hepburn

2. "She is a woman who marches to some unstruck music, unheard by the rest of us."

   writer to whom Greta Garbo gave her last interview—in 1929

3. "When I try to discover what is the indispensable quality that is necessary to become a star, I come to the conclusion that it is the *desire* to be a star."

   George Sanders, *Memoirs of a Professional Cad*

4. "So I never worked with Cooper, Gable, Grant—any of the real kings of the screen. They had their films and I had mine."

   Bette Davis to Rex Reed

5. "To be a star is to own the world and all the people in it. After a taste of stardom, everything else is poverty."

   Hedy Lamarr

6. "When I'm a star I want everybody to know it."

   Gloria Swanson

7. "It was all beauty and it was all talent; and if you had it they protected you."

   Lana Turner

8. "I shall ride the parade in a platinum car,
   My features will shine, my name will be star,
   Day long and night long the bells I shall peal,

And down the long street I shall turn the cart-wheel."
W.H. Auden

9. "I'm goin' to Hollywood—goin' to be discovuhed."
Marilyn Monroe in *Bus Stop*

10. "The thirst for applause, if the last infirmity of noble minds,
is also the first infirmity of weak ones."
John Ruskin

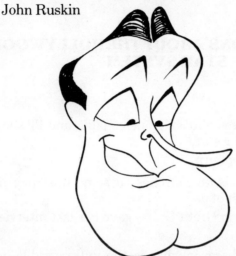

10 UNFORGETTABLE MOVIE ENDINGS

1. An ex-schoolmaster staggers back to his old classroom to die—
The Blue Angel (1930), with Marlene Dietrich and Emil
Jannings.

2. A soldier in the act of reaching for a butterfly is shot dead—
All Quiet on the Western Front (1930), with Lew Ayres.

3. A woman stands on the prow of a ship and sails into exile with
a man's body lying at her side— *Queen Christina* (1933), with
Greta Garbo and John Gilbert.

4. A tramp and a girl walk up a country road leading into the
hills— *Modern Times* (1936), with Charles Chaplin and Paulette Goddard.

5. A girl wakes up in bed to find herself surrounded by her aunt
and uncle, three farm hands, and a travelling showman— *The
Wizard of Oz* (1939), with Judy Garland, Bert Lahr, and Ray
Bolger.

218

6. A monogrammed pillow is consumed by fire— *Rebecca* (1940), with Joan Fontaine, Laurence Olivier, George Sanders, and Judith Anderson.

7. Police take a woman to an elevator; it descends and the hero walks away— *The Maltese Falcon* (1941), with Humphrey Bogart and Peter Lorre.

8. Two men walk away from the camera across a dark airport landing strip— *Casablanca* (1942), with Humphrey Bogart, Ingrid Bergman, Paul Henreid, and Peter Lorre.

9. A man and a woman approach each other on a quiet lane near a cemetery, but pass without speaking— *The Third Man* (1949), with Orson Welles, Joseph Cotten, Valli, and Trevor Howard.

10. A woman paces mournfully down a railway station platform when suddenly a man appears out of the crowd. They embrace— *A Man and a Woman* (1966), with Jean Louis Trintignant and Anouk Aimée.

10 MEMORABLE LINES FROM THE MOVIES

1. "Frankly my dear, I don't give a damn."
   Clark Gable to Vivien Leigh in *Gone With the Wind* (1939)

2. "I'm asking you to marry me, you little fool."
   Laurence Olivier to Joan Fontaine in *Rebecca* (1940)

3. "Yes, I killed him. And I'm glad, I tell you. Glad, glad, glad!"
   Bette Davis to Herbert Marshall in *The Letter* (1941)

4. "If you want anything, just whistle . . . "
   Lauren Bacall to Humphrey Bogart in *To Have and Have Not* (1944)

5. "I never dreamed that any mere physical experience could be so stimulating."
   Katharine Hepburn to Humphrey Bogart in *The African Queen* (1951)

6. "Call me Sausage."
   Joyce Grenfell to Lloyd Lamble in *Blue Murder at St. Trinian's* (1952)

7. "Would you like a leg or a breast?"
   Grace Kelly to Cary Grant in *To Catch a Thief* (1955)

8. "Your idea of fidelity is not having more than one man in bed at the same time."
   Dirk Bogarde to Julie Christie in *Darling* (1965)

9. "Well, Tillie, when the hell are we going to get some dinner?"
   Spencer Tracy's last line to Katharine Hepburn in *Guess Who's Coming to Dinner?* (1967)

10. "She cut off her nipples with garden shears. You call that normal?"
    Elizabeth Taylor to Marlon Brando in *Reflections in a Golden Eye* (1968)

Ginger Rogers and Fred Astaire—almost certainly one of the screen's most romantic couples.

10 OF THE SCREEN'S MOST ROMANTIC COUPLES

1. Elizabeth Taylor and Richard Burton
2. Jeanette MacDonald and Nelson Eddy
3. Katharine Hepburn and Spencer Tracy
4. Ginger Rogers and Fred Astaire
5. Betty Grable and Dan Dailey
6. Lauren Bacall and Humphrey Bogart
7. Olivia de Havilland and Errol Flynn
8. Diane Keaton and Woody Allen
9. Judy Garland and Mickey Rooney
10. Julie Christie and Warren Beatty

10 ROMANTIC NOVELS THAT BECAME ROMANTIC FILMS

1. *The Barretts of Wimpole Street* by T. Beiser

   A biography of Elizabeth Barrett and Robert Browning was made into a movie in 1934, starring Merle Oberon and Laurence Olivier, remade in 1957 starring Jennifer Jones and John Gielgud.

2. *Wuthering Heights* by Emily Brontë

   Merle Oberon as Catherine and Laurence Olivier as Heathcliff are the star-crossed lovers in the 1939 movie classic.

3. *Pride and Prejudice* by Jane Austen

   The 1940 movie stars Laurence Olivier as Darcy and Greer Garson as Elizabeth.

4. *Jane Eyre* by Charlotte Bronte

   The artistically successful 1944 movie stars Orson Welles as Rochester and Joan Fontaine as Jane.

5. *Great Expectations* by Charles Dickens

   John Mills plays Pip; Valerie Hobson, Estella (as adults) in the 1946 movie of Dickens' great classic.

6. *War and Peace* by Leo Tolstoy

   Audrey Hepburn as Natasha and Mel Ferrer as Andrei are beautifully matched in the epic 1956 movie.

7. *The Sun Also Rises* by Ernest Hemingway

   The movie, made in 1957, stars Tyrone Power as Jake and Ava Gardner as Lady Brett Ashley.

8. *Room at the Top* by John Braine

   The 1959 movie stars Simone Signoret as the bored Alice Aisgill and Laurence Harvey as the social-climbing Joe Lampton.

9. *Dr. Zhivago* by Boris Pasternak

   The 1965 movie stars Julie Christie as Lara and Omar Sharif as Zhivago.

10. *Women in Love* by D.H. Lawrence

    Glenda Jackson is a compelling Gudrun in the 1969 movie. Oliver Reed plays Gerald.

Julie Christie has teamed up with Warren Beatty to become one of the screen's most romantic couples.

10 MOVIES ABOUT BALLET

1. *Dance, Girl, Dance* (1940) with Maureen O'Hara, Lucille Ball, and Maria Ouspenskaya.

    A young girl wants to become a ballerina but is pushed into burlesque.

2. *The Specter of the Rose* (1946) with Judith Anderson, Ivan Kirov, and Viola Essen

    An insane ballet dancer is accused of murder.

3. *The Unfinished Dance* (1947) with Margaret O'Brien, Cyd Charisse, and Danny Thomas.

    The sugary story of a young dancer who idolizes an older ballerina.

4. *Red Shoes* (1948) with Moira Shearer and Marius Goring.

    A young ballerina and a neophyte composer are taken under an impressario's wing.

5. *An American in Paris* (1951) with Gene Kelly and Leslie Caron.

    Joyous Gershwin music and beautiful choreography.

6. *The Band Wagon* (1953) with Fred Astaire and Cyd Charisse.

    Astaire's "Shine on Your Shoes" number is one of his best.

7. *Invitation to the Dance* (1954) with Gene Kelly.

    An ambitious but commercially unsuccessful film that tells three stories entirely in dance.

8. *Knock on Wood* (1954) with Danny Kaye and Mai Zetterling.

    Danny Kaye finds himself in a corps de ballet while unravelling an international spy intrigue.

9. *The Turning Point* (1977) with Mikhail Baryshnikov, Leslie Browne, Shirley MacLaine, and Anne Bancroft.

    Two ballet dancers are reunited after many years—one has become world famous, the other has chosen to have a family.

10. *Slow Dancin' in the Big City* (1978) with Ann Ditchburn.

    The story of a dying ballet dancer's final love.

10 WELL-KNOWN EARLY CLARK GABLE MOVIES

1. *No Man of Her Own* (1932)
2. *It Happened One Night* (1934)
3. *China Seas* (1935)
4. *Cain and Mabel* (1936)
5. *San Francisco* (1936)
6. *Too Hot to Handle* (1938)
7. *Gone With the Wind* (1939)
8. *The Hucksters* (1947)
9. *Across the Wide Missouri* (1951)
10. *Lone Star* (1952)

10 PLAYS THAT BECAME MOVIES UNDER OTHER TITLES

1. *Amy Jolly* became *Morocco* (1938)
2. *Diamond Lil* became *She Done Him Wrong* (1933)
3. *Heaven Can Wait* became *Here Comes Mr. Jordan* and back to *Heaven Can Wait* (1978)
4. *Everybody Comes to Rick's* became *Casablanca* (1942)
5. *Joan of Lorraine* became *Joan of Arc* (1948)
6. *Washington Square* became *The Heiress* (1949)
7. *Green Grow the Lilacs* became *Oklahoma* (1955)
8. *The Sleeping Princess* became *The Prince and the Showgirl* (1957)
9. *The Time of the Cuckoo* became *Summertime* (1955)
10. *Matilda Shouted Fire* became *Midnight Lace* (1960)

10 MOVIES ABOUT WORLD WAR II

1. *A Wing and a Prayer* (1943)
    with Don Ameche and Dana Andrews
2. *Sahara* (1943)
    with Humphrey Bogart and Lloyd Bridges
3. *Air Force* (1943)
    with John Garfield and Gig Young
4. *So Proudly We Hail* (1943)
    with Claudette Colbert, Paulette Goddard, Veronica Lake
5. *The Moon Is Down* (1943)
    with Cedric Hardwicke and Lee J. Cobb
6. *The Story of Dr. Wassell* (1944)
    with Gary Cooper and Dennis O'Keefe
7. *Objective Burma* (1945)
    with Errol Flynn
8. *Command Decision* (1949)
    with Clark Gable and Walter Pidgeon
9. *Twelve O'Clock High* (1950)
    with Gregory Peck
10. *An American Guerilla in the Philippines* (1950)
    with Tyrone Power

10 STARS WHO NARRATED STORIES IN THEIR MOVIES

1. Flora Robson in *Wuthering Heights* (1939)
2. Joan Fontaine in *Rebecca* (1940)
3. Charles Boyer in *Hold Back the Dawn* (1941)

226

4. George Montgomery in *Roxie Hart* (1942)

5. Herbert Marshall in *The Razor's Edge* (1946)

6. Humphrey Bogart in *Dead Reckoning* (1947)

7. Dennis Price in *Kind Hearts and Coronets* (1949)

8. Spencer Tracy in *Edward My Son* (1949)

9. Alec Guinness in *The Lavender Hill Mob* (1950)

10. Marlon Brando in *The Teahouse of the August Moon* (1956)

10 MOVIES ABOUT BASEBALL

1. *Alibi Ike* (1935)

2. *The Kid from Cleveland* (1949)

3. *It Happens Every Spring* (1949)

4. *Take Me Out to the Ball Game* (1949)

5. *The Stratton Story* (1949)

6. *The Jackie Robinson Story* (1950)

7. *Angels in the Outfield* (1951)

8. *Damn Yankees* (1958)

9. *Bad News Bears* (1976)

10. *The Bad News Bears in Breaking Training* (1977)

10 ROLES PLAYED BY THE SAME STARS IN DIFFERENT MOVIES

1. The Scarlet Pimpernel by Leslie Howard, Barry K. Barnes, David Niven
2. Dr. Jekyll and Mr. Hyde by John Barrymore, Fredric March, Spencer Tracy
3. Disraeli by John Gielgud, George Arliss, Alec Guinness
4. The Devil by Ray Milland, Walter Houston, Laird Cregar
5. Calamity Jane by Yvonne de Carlo, Doris Day, Jean Arthur
6. Henry the Eighth by Montagu Love, Charles Laughton, Sidney James
7. Wyatt Earp by James Garner, Burt Lancaster, Henry Fonda
8. Adolf Hitler by Bobby Watson, Luther Adler, Richard Baseheart
9. Death by Cedric Hardwicke, Maria Casares, Fredric March
10. Queen Victoria by Irene Dunne, Anna Nagle, Fay Compton

10 ACTORS WHO PLAYED "THE MAN" IN MOVIES

1. Ronald Colman in *The Man who Broke the Bank at Monte Carlo* (1935)
2. James Mason in *The Man in Gray* (1945)
3. Alec Guinness in *The Man in the White Suit* (1952)
4. Glenn Ford in *The Man from the Alamo* (1953)
5. James Stewart in *The Man from Laramie* (1955)
6. Frank Sinatra in *The Man with the Golden Arm* (1955)
7. Kirk Douglas in *The Man without a Star* (1955)
8. Gregory Peck in *The Man in the Gray Flannel Suit* (1956)
9. Henry Fonda in *The Man who Understood Women* (1959)
10. Burt Reynolds in *The Man who Loved Cat Dancing* (1973)

10 WELL-KNOWN "JOHNNY" FILMS

1. *Johnny Eager* (1941)
2. *Johnny Come Lately* (1943)
3. *Johnny Belinda* (1948)
4. *Johnny Allegro* (1949)
5. *Johnny Dark* (1954)
6. *Johnny Guitar* (1954)
7. *Johnny Concho* (1956)
8. *Johnny Tremain* (1957)
9. *No Love for Johnny* (1961)
10. *Johnny Cool* (1963)

8 FAMOUS "HEART" MOVIES

1. *None but the Lonely Heart* (1944)
2. *The Secret Heart* (1946)
3. *The Naked Heart* (1949)
4. *Kind Hearts and Coronets* (1949)
5. *The Wild Heart* (1952)
6. *The Heart of the Matter* (1954)
7. *The Heart Is a Lonely Hunter* (1968)
8. *The Heartbreak Kid* (1972)

Buster Keaton rides again.

12
HUMOR

10 OF HOLLYWOOD'S MOST HUMOROUS QUOTATIONS

1. "After *The Wizard of Oz* I was typecast as a lion, and there aren't all that many parts for lions."
   Bert Lahr

2. "There is only one thing that can kill the movies and that is education."
   Will Rogers

3. "Scratch an actor—and you'll find an actress."
   Dorothy Parker

4. "We have all passed a lot of water since then."
   Samuel Goldwyn

5. "Fish f--- in it."
   W.C. Fields, on being asked why he never drank water

6. "The real, real reason I like to be in movies is because it's an easy place to have hems done. There's always a seamstress on the set. And if you break a chair, they can fix it—they have people who can do anything. Chair people, hem people."
   Barbra Streisand

7. "I'm feeling a little tired today. One of those fellows will have to go home."
   Mae West, on arriving at her office and being greeted by a group of young men

8. "The trouble is that you are only interested in art, and I am only interested in money."
   George Bernard Shaw to Samuel Goldwyn, while negotiating to film one of Shaw's plays

9. "Jack Warner has oilcloth pockets so he can steal soup."
   Wilson Mizner

10. "Tell me, how did you love the picture?"
    attributed to Samuel Goldwyn

13 FAMOUS HOLLYWOOD JOKES

1. "Don't be hard on her," a friend cautioned William Wyler about the star of *Funny Girl.* "It's the first picture Miss Streisand's ever directed."

2. Dorothy Parker squelched a drunk, who nagged her in a bar during an unpleasant period of her blacklisting in the late forties: "With the crown of thorns I wear, why should I be bothered with a prick like you?"

3. Marlon Brando was to have starred in *Lawrence of Arabia,* but Sam Spiegel wanted a new face for Lawrence. He created a new star—Peter O'Toole. Afterwards, without naming any names, Sam said, "You make a star, you make a monster."

4. During the late sixties when Shirley Temple was running for office in California, political posters appeared which consisted of large blow-ups of a beaming ten-year-old Shirley. Underneath were written the words: "If you don't vote for me, I'll hold my breath."

5. The most often quoted remark of Jack Warner's was made when he returned from Europe in the sixties and was told by a friend that Ronald Reagan, who had been a Warner contract player for many years, had been nominated to run for Governor of California. Warner shook his head. "No, no," he said. "Jimmy Stewart for governor—Reagan for his best friend."

6. Dorothy Parker found herself at a party where an actor, who had been appearing in London for a season, was holding forth. The actor persisted in using only British forms of speech and kept referring to his "shedule." "If you don't mind my saying so," said Miss Parker, "You're full of skit."

7. One evening Jimmy Durante was sitting between acts at a table with John Barrymore and other friends. Barrymore said to Jimmy, "You should play Hamlet."

   "The hell with them small towns," Durante replied. "I'll take New York."

8. It was after the birth of Irving Thalberg's first son that Eddie Cantor sent him a congratulatory telegram, which read: CONGRATULATIONS ON YOUR LATEST PRODUCTION. AM SURE IT WILL LOOK BETTER AFTER IT'S BEEN CUT.

9. Marlon Brando was sipping tea in the foyer of the fashionable Prince de Galles Hotel in Paris. A passing waiter inadvertently poured some boiling water on to Brando's lap. He jumped up in pain. Afterwards he said reflectively, "I'd like to write the headline for this story—Brando Scalds Balls at Prince de Galles."

10. W.C. Fields was in his dressing room at Paramount when visited by two ladies who were canvassing for donations to some worthy California charity. "I am very sorry mesdames," said Fields, "but I only give to one charity—F.E.B.F." When pressed as to what that stood for, he explained: "Fuck Everyone but Fields."

11. Jack Benny once told a London audience that he was well aware of his reputation for prudence. "It's absolutely true," he said. "I don't want to tell you how much insurance I carry with Prudential, but all I can say is—when I go, *they* go."

12. Wit and writer Dorothy Parker when asked for the third time why she had not delivered a script as promised, snapped back, "I've been too fucking busy—and vice versa."

13. When Elizabeth Taylor married her last husband and the Justice of the Peace asked for the names of her other husbands, she said, "What is this, a memory test?"

10 QUOTES OVERHEARD IN HOLLYWOOD

1. "If I need some shit from you, I'll squeeze your head."

   Kris Kristofferson to Jon Peters during production of *A Star Is Born* (1976)

2. "You've had nothing until you've had me. I am the biggest and the best. I can go all night and all day."

   Darryl Zanuck to Joan Collins

3. "No, no. Please. It's impossible. I can't. My father doesn't want me to have any babies!"

   Katharine Hepburn to John Barrymore during filming of *A Bill of Divorcement* (1932)

233

Bob Hope's forte is as a stand-up comic, and although he has been telling the same jokes for forty years, people still love them.

4. "Pass the salt. *It* isn't black!"

    Jim Brown to Raquel Welch in *100 Rifles* (1969) (off screen)

5. "I have more talent in my smallest fart than you do in your entire body."

    Walter Matthau to Barbra Streisand during filming of *Hello Dolly* (1969)

6. "If you were more of a woman, I would be more of a man. Kissing you is like kissing the side of a beer bottle."

    Laurence Harvey to Capucine, during filming of *Walk on the Wild Side* (1962)

7. "I'd wring your neck, if you had one."

    Noel Coward to Claudette Colbert

8. "Why all the fuss? I just played myself."

    Errol Flynn after *The Sun Also Rises* (1957)

9. "Gary Cooper? He's just like a horse."

    Clara Bow

10. "Any girl can look glamorous. All she has to do is stand still and look stupid."

    Hedy Lamarr

10 FAMOUS HOLLYWOOD COMICS

1. CHARLIE CHAPLIN

    Everything has already been said about the noble clown, without a doubt the greatest comic actor Hollywood has produced.

2. CAROLE LOMBARD

    She could have been a greater sex symbol than Marilyn Monroe, but her keen sense of fun and her gift for comedy made her the great comedienne of the 1930's.

The Marx Brothers great appeal lay in their flouting of authority at a time when society was much more in awe of authority than it is today.

3. WOODY ALLEN

Philosopher, playwright, comic, Woody Allen's appeal lies in his ability to make contact with his audience through their laughter.

4. JERRY LEWIS

The perennial kid, Jerry Lewis's brand of humor is either loved or hated, but even his worst enemies have to admire his mastery of comic timing and his inventive sight gags.

5. W.C. FIELDS

He thought in terms of gags rather than plots, but his face changed with every part he played. Not only a great comic, W.C. Fields was also a great actor.

6. BOB HOPE

Hope's forte is as a stand-up comic, and although he has been telling the same jokes for forty years, people still love them, probably because his character has never changed either.

7. JUDY HOLLIDAY

Judy Holliday's specialty was playing dumb blondes (*Born Yesterday, The Solid Gold Cadillac, The Marrying Kind*), but in real life she had an IQ of 172 and was a hard-driving technician, a perfectionist, and a merciless self-critic. She was also, however, a great actress and she gave the dumb blonde genre class and depth it had never had before or has had since.

8. ABBOTT AND COSTELLO

Stand-up comics Bud Abbott and Lou Costello reached the peak of their popularity in the forties, at a time when the North American taste for slapstick and exaggeration was at an all-time high.

9. THE MARX BROTHERS

The Marx Brothers great appeal lay in their flouting of authority—fearlessly and contemptuously—at a time when society was much more in awe of authority than it is today.

10. LAUREL AND HARDY

Stan Laurel and Oliver Hardy were equally successful in both silent and sound movies. Their obvious affection for each other, as well as their sweetness and gentleness, won them a very devoted following.

Betty Grable showed us How to Be Very, Very Popular *in 1955.*

10 FAMOUS "HOW TO" MOVIES

1. *How to Marry a Millionaire* (1953)
    with Marilyn Monroe, Betty Grable, and Lauren Bacall
2. *How to Be Very, Very Popular* (1955)
    with Betty Grable, Robert Cummings, and Charles Coburn
3. *How to Stuff a Wild Bikini* (1965)
    with Annette Funicello, Buster Keaton, and Mickey Rooney
4. *How to Steal a Million* (1966)
    with Audrey Hepburn and Peter O'Toole
5. *How to Succeed in Business without Really Trying* (1967)
    with Robert Morse and Rudy Vallee
6. *How to Murder Your Wife* (1968)
    with Jack Lemmon and Virna Lisi
7. *How to Save a Marriage (and Ruin Your Life)* (1968)
    with Dean Martin and Eli Wallach
8. *How to Commit Marriage* (1969)
    with Bob Hope and Jackie Gleason
9. *How to Steal an Airplane* (1971)
    with Claudine Longet
10. *How to Break Up a Happy Divorce* (1976)
    with Barbara Eden

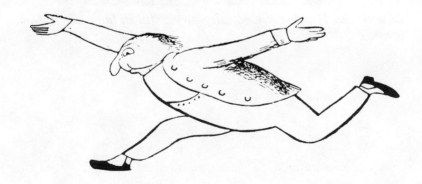

Laurel and Hardy were equally successful in both silent and sound comedies.

13
AWARDS

5 GREAT QUOTES ON ACTING

1. "You spend all your life trying to do something they put people in asylums for."
   Jane Fonda

2. "The only thing you owe the public is a good performance."
   Humphrey Bogart

3. "They made me sound as if I'd been castrated."
   Tallulah Bankhead, complaining about the talkies

4. "There are lots of methods. Mine involves a lot of talent, a glass, and some cracked ice."
   John Barrymore

5. "The Oscar means one thing—an added million-dollar gross for the picture. It's a big publicity contest. Oh, the voting is legitimate, but there's the sentimentality. One year when Elizabeth Taylor got a hole in her throat, I cancelled my plane reservations."
   Shirley MacLaine

Vivien Leigh won Oscars for both Gone With the Wind *(1939) and* A Streetcar Named Desire *(1951).*

THE 10 ACTRESSES WHO HAVE WON THE MOST ACADEMY AWARDS

1. KATHARINE HEPBURN—3
   Morning Glory (1932)
   Guess Who's Coming to Dinner (1967)
   The Lion in Winter (1968)

2. INGRID BERGMAN—3
   Gaslight (1944)
   Anastasia (1956)
   Murder on the Orient Express (1974) (Best Supporting Actress)

3. BETTE DAVIS—2
   Dangerous (1935)
   Jezebel (1938)

4. LUISE RAINER—2
   The Great Ziegfeld (1936)
   The Good Earth (1937)

5. VIVIEN LEIGH—2
   Gone With the Wind (1939)
   A Streetcar Named Desire (1951)

6. ELIZABETH TAYLOR—2
   Butterfield 8 (1960)
   Who's Afraid of Virginia Woolf (1966)

7. OLIVIA DE HAVILLAND—2
   To Each His Own (1946)
   The Heiress (1949)

8. GLENDA JACKSON—2
   Women in Love (1970)
   A Touch of Class (1973)

9. JANE FONDA—2
   Klute (1971)
   Coming Home (1979)

10. HELEN HAYES—2
    The Sin of Madelon Claudet (1931)
    Airport (1970) (Best Supporting Actress)

Olivia de Havilland is one of eight actresses to have won two Academy Awards.

10 FAMOUS ACTRESSES WHO HAVE NEVER WON AN ACADEMY AWARD

1. Greta Garbo
2. Marlene Dietrich
3. Mae West
4. Gloria Swanson
5. Shirley Temple

6. Marilyn Monroe
7. Judy Garland
8. Ava Gardner
9. Doris Day
10. Jacqueline Bissett

7 ACTORS WHO HAVE WON MORE THAN ONE ACADEMY AWARD

1. WALTER BRENNAN—3 (For Best Supporting Actor)
   Come and Get It (1936)
   Kentucky (1938)
   The Westerner (1940)

2. FREDERIC MARCH—2
   Dr. Jekyll and Mr. Hyde (1931)
   The Best Years of Our Lives (1946)

3. SPENCER TRACY—2
   Captains Courageous (1937)
   Boys Town (1938)

4. GARY COOPER—2
   Sergeant York (1941)
   High Noon (1952)

5. MARLON BRANDO—2
   On the Waterfront (1954)
   The Godfather (1972)

6. ANTHONY QUINN—2 (For Best Supporting Actor)
   Viva Zapata! (1952)
   Lust for Life (1956)

7. PETER USTINOV—2 (For Best Supporting Actor)
   Spartacus (1960)
   Topkapi (1964)

10 FAMOUS ACTORS WHO HAVE NEVER WON AN ACADEMY AWARD (FOR ACTING)

1. Charlie Chaplin
2. Richard Burton
3. Paul Newman
4. Robert Redford
5. Henry Fonda
6. Cary Grant
7. Warren Beatty
8. Elvis Presley
9. Rudolph Valentino
10. Bob Hope

3 AWARD WINNERS OF THE 1920'S FOR BEST ACTRESS

1. 1927 Janet Gaynor for *Seventh Heaven, Street Angel,* and *Sunrise*
2. 1928 Mary Pickford for *Coquette*
3. 1929 Norma Shearer for *The Divorcée*

3 ACADEMY AWARD WINNERS OF THE 1920'S FOR BEST ACTOR

1. 1927 Emil Jannings for *The Last Command* and *The Way of All Flesh*
2. 1928 Warner Baxter for *Old Arizona*
3. 1929 George Arliss for *Disraeli*

3 ACADEMY AWARD WINNERS OF THE 1920'S FOR BEST PICTURE

1. 1927 *Wings*
2. 1928 *Broadway Melody*
3. 1929 *All Quiet on the Western Front*

9 ACADEMY AWARD WINNERS OF THE 1930'S FOR BEST ACTRESS

1. 1930 Marie Dressler for *Min and Bill*
2. 1931 Helen Hayes for *The Sin of Madelon Claudet*
3. 1932 Katharine Hepburn for *Morning Glory*
   1933 No award
4. 1934 Claudette Colbert in *It Happened One Night*
5. 1935 Bette Davis in *Dangerous*
6. 1936 Luise Rainer for *The Great Ziegfeld*
7. 1937 Luise Rainer for *The Good Earth*
8. 1938 Bette Davis for *Jezebel*
9. 1939 Vivien Leigh for *Gone With the Wind*

10 ACADEMY AWARD WINNERS OF THE 1930'S FOR BEST ACTOR

1. 1930 Lionel Barrymore for *A Free Soul*
2. 1931 Fredric March for *Dr. Jekyll and Mr. Hyde*
3. Wallace Beery for *The Champ*
4. 1932 Charles Laughton for *The Private Life of Henry VIII*
   1933 no award
5. 1934 Clark Gable for *It Happened One Night*
6. 1935 Victor McLaglen for *The Informer*
7. 1936 Paul Muni for *The Story of Louis Pasteur*
8. 1937 Spencer Tracy for *Captains Courageous*
9. 1938 Spencer Tracy for *Boys Town*
10. 1939 Robert Donat for *Goodbye Mr. Chips*

9 ACADEMY AWARD WINNERS OF THE 1930'S FOR BEST PICTURE

1. 1930 *Cimarron*
2. 1931 *Grand Hotel*
3. 1932 *Cavalcade*
   1933 no award
4. 1934 *It Happened One Night*
5. 1935 *Mutiny on the Bounty*
6. 1936 *The Great Ziegfeld*
7. 1937 *The Life of Emile Zola*
8. 1938 *You Can't Take It With You*
9. 1939 *Gone With the Wind*

10 ACADEMY AWARD WINNERS OF THE 1940's FOR BEST ACTRESS

1. 1940 Ginger Rogers for *Kitty Foyle*
2. 1941 Joan Fontaine for *Suspicion*
3. 1942 Greer Garson for *Mrs. Miniver*
4. 1943 Jennifer Jones for *Song of Bernadette*
5. 1944 Ingrid Bergman for *Gaslight*
6. 1945 Joan Crawford for *Mildred Pierce*
7. 1946 Olivia de Havilland for *To Each His Own*
8. 1947 Loretta Young for *The Farmer's Daughter*
9. 1948 Jane Wyman for *Johnny Belinda*
10. 1949 Olivia de Havilland for *The Heiress*

10 ACADEMY AWARD WINNERS OF THE 1940'S
FOR BEST ACTOR

1. 1940 James Stewart for *The Philadelphia Story*
2. 1941 Gary Cooper for *Sergeant York*
3. 1942 James Cagney for *Yankee Doodle Dandy*
4. 1943 Paul Lukas for *Watch on the Rhine*
5. 1944 Bing Crosby for *Going My Way*
6. 1945 Ray Milland for *The Lost Weekend*
7. 1946 Fredric March for *The Best Years of Our Lives*
8. 1947 Ronald Coleman for *A Double Life*
9. 1948 Laurence Olivier for *Hamlet*
10. 1949 Broderick Crawford for *All the King's Men*

10 ACADEMY AWARD WINNERS OF THE 1940'S
FOR BEST PICTURE

1. 1940 *Rebecca*
2. 1941 *How Green Was My Valley*
3. 1942 *Mrs. Miniver*
4. 1943 *Casablanca*
5. 1944 *Going My Way*
6. 1945 *The Lost Weekend*
7. 1946 *The Best Years of Our Lives*
8. 1947 *Gentleman's Agreement*
9. 1948 *Hamlet*
10. 1949 *All the King's Men*

10 ACADEMY AWARD WINNERS OF THE 1950'S FOR BEST ACTRESS

1. 1950 Judy Holliday for *Born Yesterday*
2. 1951 Vivien Leigh for *A Streetcar Named Desire*
3. 1952 Shirley Booth for *Come Back, Little Sheba*
4. 1953 Audrey Hepburn for *Roman Holiday*
5. 1954 Grace Kelly for *The Country Girl*
6. 1955 Anna Magnani for *The Rose Tattoo*
7. 1956 Ingrid Bergman for *Anastasia*
8. 1957 Joanne Woodward for *The Three Faces of Eve*
9. 1958 Susan Hayward for *I Want to Live*
10. 1959 Simone Signoret for *Room at the Top*

10 ACADEMY AWARD WINNERS OF THE 1950'S FOR BEST ACTOR

1. 1950 José Ferrer for *Cyrano de Bergerac*
2. 1951 Humphrey Bogart for *The African Queen*
3. 1952 Gary Cooper for *High Noon*
4. 1953 William Holden for *Stalag 17*
5. 1954 Marlon Brando for *On the Waterfront*
6. 1955 Ernest Borgnine for *Marty*
7. 1956 Yul Brynner for *The King and I*
8. 1957 Alec Guinness for *The Bridge on the River Kwai*
9. 1958 David Niven for *Separate Tables*
10. 1959 Charlton Heston for *Ben-Hur*

10 ACADEMY AWARD WINNERS OF THE 1950'S FOR BEST PICTURE

1. 1950 *All About Eve*
2. 1951 *An American in Paris*
3. 1952 *The Greatest Show on Earth*
4. 1953 *From Here to Eternity*
5. 1954 *On the Waterfront*
6. 1955 *Marty*
7. 1956 *Around the World in 80 Days*
8. 1957 *The Bridge on the River Kwai*
9. 1958 *Gigi*
10. 1959 *Ben-Hur*

11 ACADEMY AWARDS OF THE 1960's FOR BEST ACTRESS

1. 1960 Elizabeth Taylor for *Butterfield 8*
2. 1961 Sophia Loren for *Two Women*
3. 1962 Anne Bancroft for *The Miracle Worker*
4. 1963 Patricia Neal for *Hud*
5. 1964 Julie Andrews for *Mary Poppins*
6. 1965 Julie Christie for *Darling*
7. 1966 Elizabeth Taylor for *Who's Afraid of Virginia Woolf?*
8. 1967 Katharine Hepburn for *Guess Who's Coming to Dinner?*
9. 1968 Katharine Hepburn for *The Lion in Winter*
10. 1968 Barbra Streisand for *Funny Girl*
11. 1969 Maggie Smith for *The Prime of Miss Jean Brodie*

10 ACADEMY AWARD WINNERS OF THE 1960'S FOR BEST ACTOR

1. 1960 Burt Lancaster for *Elmer Gantry*
2. 1961 Maximilian Schell for *Judgment at Nuremberg*
3. 1962 Gregory Peck for *To Kill a Mockingbird*
4. 1963 Sidney Poitier for *Lilies of the Field*
5. 1964 Rex Harrison for *My Fair Lady*
6. 1965 Lee Marvin for *Cat Ballou*
7. 1966 Paul Scofield for *A Man for All Seasons*
8. 1967 Rod Steiger for *In the Heat of the Night*
9. 1968 Cliff Robertson for *Charly*
10. 1969 John Wayne for *True Grit*

10 ACADEMY AWARD WINNERS OF THE 1960'S FOR BEST PICTURE

1. 1960 *The Apartment*
2. 1961 *West Side Story*
3. 1962 *Lawrence of Arabia*
4. 1963 *Tom Jones*
5. 1964 *My Fair Lady*
6. 1965 *The Sound of Music*
7. 1966 *A Man for All Seasons*
8. 1967 *In the Heat of the Night*
9. 1968 *Oliver*
10. 1969 *Midnight Cowboy*

Jack Lemmon won an Oscar for his role in Save the Tiger *in 1973.*

9 ACADEMY AWARD WINNERS OF THE 1970's FOR BEST ACTRESS

1. 1970 Glenda Jackson for *Women in Love*
2. 1971 Jane Fonda for *Klute*
3. 1972 Liza Minnelli for *Cabaret*
4. 1973 Glenda Jackson for *A Touch of Class*
5. 1974 Ellen Burstyn for *Alice Doesn't Live Here Anymore*
6. 1975 Louise Fletcher for *One Flew Over the Cuckoo's Nest*
7. 1976 Faye Dunaway for *Network*
8. 1977 Diane Keaton for *Annie Hall*
9. 1978 Jane Fonda for *Coming Home*

9 ACADEMY AWARD WINNERS OF THE 1970's FOR BEST ACTOR

1. 1970 George C. Scott for *Patton* (award declined)
2. 1971 Gene Hackman for *The French Connection*
3. 1972 Marlon Brando for *The Godfather* (award declined)
4. 1973 Jack Lemmon for *Save the Tiger*
5. 1974 Art Carney for *Harry and Tonto*
6. 1975 Jack Nicholson for *One Flew Over the Cuckoo's Nest*
7. 1976 Peter Finch for *Network*
8. 1977 Richard Dreyfuss for *The Goodbye Girl*
9. 1978 Jon Voight for *Coming Home*

254

9 ACADEMY AWARD WINNERS OF THE 1970'S FOR BEST PICTURE

1. 1970 *Patton*
2. 1971 *The French Connection*
3. 1972 *The Godfather*
4. 1973 *The Sting*
5. 1974 *The Godfather Part II*
6. 1975 *One Flew Over the Cuckoo's Nest*
7. 1976 *Rocky*
8. 1977 *Annie Hall*
9. 1978 *Deer Hunter*

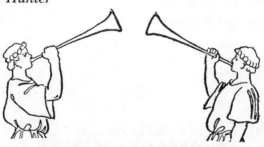

9 ACADEMY AWARD WINNERS OF THE 1970'S FOR BEST FOREIGN LANGUAGE FILM

1. 1970 *Investigation of a Citizen Above Suspicion* (Italy)
2. 1971 *The Garden of the Finzi-Continis* (Italy)
3. 1972 *The Discreet Charm of the Bourgeoisie* (France)
4. 1973 *Day for Night* (France)
5. 1974 *Amarcord* (Italy)
6. 1975 *Dersu Uzala* (U.S.S.R.)
7. 1976 *Black and White in Color* (Ivory Coast)
8. 1977 *Madame Rosa* (France)
9. 1978 *Get Out Your Handkerchiefs* (France)

11 CANNES FILM FESTIVAL AWARDS FOR BEST MOVIES OF THE 1960'S

1. 1960 *La Dolce Vita* (Italy)
2. 1961 *Viridiana* (Spain)
3. 1961 *Une aussi longue* (France)
4. 1962 *The Given Word* (Brazil)
5. 1963 *The Leopard* (Italy)
6. 1964 *The Umbrellas of Cherbourg* (France)
7. 1965 *The Knack* (England)
8. 1966 *A Man and a Woman* (France)
9. 1966 *Signore e Signori* (Italy)
10. 1967 *Blow-Up* (England)
    1968 No awards
11. 1969 *If* (England)

13 CANNES FILM FESTIVAL AWARDS FOR BEST MOVIES OF THE 1970'S

1. 1970 *M*A*S*H** (U.S.A.)
2. 1971 *The Go-Between* (England)
3. 1972 *The Working Class Goes to Paradise* (Italy)
4. 1972 *The Mattei Affair* (Italy)
5. 1973 *Scarecrow* (U.S.A.)
6. 1973 *The Hireling* (England)
7. 1974 *The Conversation* (U.S.A.)
8. 1975 *Chronicle of the Burning Years* (Algeria)
9. 1976 *Taxi Driver* (U.S.A.)
10. 1977 *Padre Padrone* (Italy)

11. 1978 *The Tree of the Wooden Clogs* (Italy)

12. 1979 *Apocalypse Now* (U.S.A.)

13. 1979 *The Tin Drum* (Germany)

10 SONGS SUNG BY OSCAR WINNERS

1. "Moon River," sung by Audrey Hepburn in *Breakfast at Tiffany's* (1961)

2. "Someone to Watch Over Me," sung by Julie Andrews in *Star!* (1968)

3. "True Love," sung by Grace Kelly in *High Society* (1956)

4. "Who Wants to Be a Millionaire," sung by Celeste Holm in *High Society* (1956)

5. "I've Grown Accustomed to Her Face," sung by Rex Harrison in *My Fair Lady* (1964)

6. "Poor Jud Is Dead," sung by Rod Steiger in *Oklahoma!* (1955)

7. "I Couldn't Sleep a Wink Last Night," sung by Frank Sinatra in *Higher and Higher* (1943)

8. "Shanghai Lil," sung by James Cagney in *Footlight Parade* (1933)

9. "If I Loved You," sung by Shirley Jones in *Carousel* (1956)

10. "They're Either Too Young or Too Old," sung by Bette Davis in *Thank Your Lucky Stars* (1943)

Orson Welles created Citizen Kane *in 1941—perhaps the best movie ever made.*

14
THE BEST AND THE WORST

10 OF HOLLYWOOD'S WORST QUOTES

1. "A team effort is a lot of people doing what I say."
   Michael Winner

2. "Never let that bastard in here—unless we need him!"
   attributed to L.B. Mayer, Jack Warner, Adolph Zukor, Harry Cohn, and others

3. "Clark Gable took the humor and sex from the characters he played."
   Joan Crawford

4. "Any of my indiscretions were with people, not actresses."
   Darryl F. Zanuck

5. "I don't like watching rape and violence in the cinema. I get enough of them at home!"
   Peter Cook

6. "Anyone who hates small dogs and children can't be all bad."
   W.C. Fields

7. "I have no further use for America. I wouldn't go back there if Jesus Christ was President."
   Charlie Chaplin

8. "Actors? Cattle."
   Alfred Hitchcock

9. "Warner Brothers is like fucking a porcupine—it's one hundred pricks against one."
   Wilson Mizner

10. "A verbal contract isn't worth the paper it's written on."
    Samuel Goldwyn

THE 10 GREATEST AMERICAN FILMS OF ALL TIME

1. *Gone with the Wind* (1939)
   with Vivien Leigh and Clark Gable

2. *Citizen Kane* (1941)
   with Orson Welles

3. *Casablanca* (1942)
   with Humphrey Bogart and Ingrid Bergman

4. *The African Queen* (1952)
   with Humphrey Bogart and Katharine Hepburn

5. *The Grapes of Wrath* (1940)
   with Henry Fonda and John Carradine

6. *One Flew Over the Cuckoo's Nest* (1975)
   with Jack Nicholson and Louise Fletcher

7. *Singin' in the Rain* (1952)
   with Gene Kelly, Debbie Reynolds, and Donald O'Connor

8. *Star Wars* (1977)
   with Mark Hamill and Alec Guinness

9. *2001: A Space Odyssey* (1968)
   with Keir Dullea and Gary Lockwood

10. *The Wizard of Oz* (1939)
    with Judy Garland, Bert Lahr, Ray Bolger, and Jack Haley

1977 American Film Institute Survey

THE 10 BEST MOVIES EVER MADE

1. *The Battleship Potemkin* (Eisenstein, 1925)

2. *The Gold Rush* (Chaplin, 1925)

3. *The Bicycle Thief* (De Sica, 1949)

4. *City Lights* (Chaplin, 1930)

260

The late Humphrey Bogart starred with Ingrid Bergman in
Casablanca—one of the great American films made in 1942.

5. *La Grande Illusion* (Renoir, 1937)

6. *Le Million* (Clair, 1930)

7. *Greed* (Von Stroheim, 1924)

8. *Hallelujah!* (Vidor, 1929)

9. *Die Dreigroschenoper* (Pabst, 1931)

10. *Brief Encounter* (Lean, 1945)

1952 Cinémathèque Belgique Survey

THE 10 BEST MOVIES EVER MADE

1. *The Bicycle Thief* (De Sica, 1949)

2. *City Lights* (Chaplin, 1925)

3. *The Gold Rush* (Chaplin, 1925)

4. *The Battleship Potemkin* (Eisenstein, 1925)

5. *Louisiana Story* (Flaherty, 1947)

6. *Intolerance* (Griffith, 1916)

7. *Greed* (Von Stroheim, 1924)

8. *Le Jour se Leve* (Carné, 1939)

9. *The Passion of Joan of Arc* (Dreyer, 1928)

10. *Brief Encounter* (Lean, 1945)

1952 *Sight and Sound* Survey

THE 10 BEST MOVIES EVER MADE

1. *Citizen Kane* (Welles, 1941)

2. *L'Avventura* (Antonioni, 1960)

3. *La Règle du Jeu* (Renoir, 1939)

4. *Greed* (Von Stroheim, 1924)

262

5. *Ugetsu Monogatari* (Mizoguchi, 1953)

6. *The Battleship Potemkin* (Eisenstein, 1925)

7. *The Bicycle Thief* (De Sica, 1949)

8. *Ivan the Terrible* (Eisenstein, 1943-46)

9. *La Terra Trema* (Visconti, 1948)

10. *L'Atalante* (Vigo, 1933)

1962 *Sight and Sound* Survey

THE 10 BEST MOVIES EVER MADE

1. *Citizen Kane* (Welles, 1941)

2. *La Règle du Jeu* (Renoir, 1939)

3. *The Battleship Potemkin* (Eisenstein, 1925)

4. *8 1/2* (Fellini, 1963)

5. *L'Avventura* (Antonioni, 1960)

6. *Persona* (Bergman, 1967)

7. *The Passion of Joan of Arc* (Dreyer, 1926)

8. *The General* (Keaton/Bruckman, 1926)

9. *The Magnificent Ambersons* (Welles, 1942)

10. *Ugetsu Monogatari* (Mizoguchi, 1953)

1972 *Sight and Sound* Survey

THE 10 MOST POPULAR MOVIES EVER TO APPEAR ON AMERICAN TELEVISION

1. *Gone With the Wind*
2. *Airport*
3. *Love Story*
4. *The Godfather Part II*
5. *The Poseidon Adventure*
6. *True Grit*
7. *The Birds*
8. *Patton*
9. *Bridge on the River Kwai*
10. *Jeremiah Johnson*

Nielsen ratings

PENELOPE GILLIATT'S 10 FAVORITE MOVIES

1. *The Navigator*
2. *La Règle du Jeu*
3. *8 1/2*
4. *Persona*
5. *Ikiru*
6. *Citizen Kane*
7. *The Apu Trilogy*
8. *The Battleship Potemkin*
9. *Jules et Jim*
10. *Weekend*

1972 *Sight and Sound* Survey

JUDITH CRIST'S 10 FAVORITE MOVIES

1. *City Lights*
2. *La Règle du Jeu*
3. *Citizen Kane*
4. *La Grande Illusion*
5. *8 1/2*
6. *La Guerre est finie*
7. *Ikiru*
8. *Winter Light*
9. *War and Peace* (Bondarchuk)
10. *The Maltese Falcon*

1972 *Sight and Sound* Survey

THE 7 BEST FILMS ABOUT WOMEN

1. *Adam's Rib* (Cukor, 1949)
2. *Persona* (Bergman)
3. *Pat and Mike* (Cukor, 1952)
4. *Celine and Julie Go Boating* (Rivette)
5. *Belle de Jour* (Bunuel, 1966)
6. *Antonia: Portrait of the Woman* (Godmilow-Collins, 1974)
7. *A Brief Vacation* (De Sica, 1975)

1975/76 *Winter Film Heritage*

MOLLY HASKELL'S 10 BEST FILMS ABOUT WOMEN

1. *Orphans of the Storm* (1922) with Lillian and Dorothy Gish
2. *Angel* (1937) with Marlene Dietrich
3. *The Major and the Minor* (1942) with Ginger Rogers
4. *Pat and Mike* (1952) with Katharine Hepburn
5. *Gentlemen Prefer Blondes* (1953) with Jane Russell and Marilyn Monroe
6. *Stromboli* (1950) with Ingrid Bergman
7. *Belle de Jour* (1966) with Catherine Deneuve
8. *My Night at Maud's* (1970) with Jean Louis Trintignant
9. *The Earrings of Madame de* (1954) with Danielle Darrieux
10. *Gertrud* (1964) directed by Carl Dreyer

1975/76 *Winter Film Heritage*

THE 10 BEST CHRISTMAS MOVIES

1. *A Christmas Carol* (1938)
2. *Holiday Inn* (1942)
3. *Christmas Holiday* (1944)
4. *Miracle on 34th Street* (1947)
5. *Black Narcissus* (1947)
6. *A Christmas Carol* (1951)
7. *The Holly and the Ivy* (1953)
8. *White Christmas* (1954)
9. *We're No Angels* (1955)
10. *Scrooge* (1970)

266

THE 6 MOST FLAGRANT EXAMPLES OF MISCASTING

1. 1970 Dean Martin for soberly piloting a 707 to a belly-landing in *Airport*
2. 1971 Elliott Gould in *The Touch*. How could Ingmar Bergman cast the boorish Gould as someone Bibi Andersson would leave Max von Sydow for?
3. 1972 Ali MacGraw as a bank robber's girlfriend on the lam in *The Getaway*.
4. 1973 Mia Farrow for being nobody's idea of Daisy Buchanan in *The Great Gatsby*.
5. 1974 Dean Martin as a clever lawyer in *Mr. Ricco*.
6. 1975 Sean Connery in *The Man Who Would Be King* for being anyone but James Bond.

The Harvard Lampoon

THE 7 WORST ACTRESSES OF THE 1970'S

1. 1970 Ali MacGraw in *Love Story*
2. 1971 Candice Bergen in *T.R. Baskin*
3. 1972 Ali MacGraw in *Getaway*
4. 1973 Barbra Streisand in *The Way We Were*
5. 1974 Julie Andrews in *The Tamarind Seed*
6. 1975 Diana Ross in *Mahogany*
7. 1976 Barbra Streisand in *A Star Is Born*

The Harvard Lampoon

THE 7 WORST ACTORS OF THE 1970'S

1. 1970 Elliott Gould in *Getting Straight*
2. 1971 Jack Nicholson in *Carnal Knowledge*
3. 1972 Robert Redford in *The Candidate*
4. 1973 Jack Lemmon in *Save the Tiger*
5. 1974 Burt Reynolds in *The Longest Yard*
6. 1975 Ryan O'Neal in *Barry Lyndon*
7. 1976 Clint Eastwood in *Dirty Harry*

The Harvard Lampoon

THE 9 WORST ACTRESSES OF THE 1960'S

1. 1960 Eva Marie Saint in *Exodus*
2. 1961 Susan Hayward in *Ada* and in *Back Street*
3. 1962 Jane Fonda in *The Chapman Report*
4. 1963 Debbie Reynolds in *How the West Was Won* and in *Mary, Mary*
5. 1964 Carroll Baker in *The Carpetbaggers*
   1965 No award
6. 1966 Ursula Andress in *Casino Royale*
7. 1967 Raquel Welch in *The Biggest Bundle of Them All*
8. 1968 Barbra Streisand in *Funny Girl*
9. 1969 Jane Fonda in *Spirits of the Dead*

The Harvard Lampoon

THE 9 WORST ACTORS OF THE 1960'S

1. 1960 Frank Sinatra in *Can-Can*
2. 1961 Richard Beymer in *West Side Story*
3. 1962 Charlton Heston in *Diamond Head,* and in *The Pigeon that Took Rome*
4. 1963 Burt Lancaster in *The Leopard* and in *Seven Days in May*
5. 1964 James Franciscus in *Youngblood Hawke*
   1965 No award
6. 1966 George Peppard in *The Blue Max*
7. 1967 Richard Burton in *Doctor Faustus* and *The Comedians*
8. 1968 Sidney Poitier in *For Love of Ivy*
9. 1969 Peter Fonda in *Easy Rider*

The Harvard Lampoon

THE 10 WORST ACTRESSES OF THE 1950'S

1. 1950 Elizabeth Taylor in *The Conspirators*
2. 1951 Corinne Calvet in *On the Riviera*
3. 1952 Marilyn Monroe in *Niagara*
4. 1953 Terry Moore in *Beneath the 12-Mile Reef*
5. 1954 Barbara Stanwyck in *Cattle Queen of Montana*
6. 1955 Debbie Reynolds in *Hit the Deck*
7. 1956 Jennifer Jones in *The Man in the Gray Flannel Suit*
8. 1957 Kim Novak in *Pal Joey* and in *Jeanne Eagels*
9. 1958 Rita Hayworth in *Separate Tables*
10. 1959 Lana Turner in *Imitation of Life*

The Harvard Lampoon

Elizabeth Taylor (with Gene Kelly) was voted one of the worst actresses of the fifties by the Harvard Lampoon.

THE 9 WORST ACTORS OF THE 1950'S

1. 1950 Clifton Webb in *Cheaper by the Dozen*
2. 1951 Robert Taylor in *Quo Vadis*
3. 1952 Jerry Lewis in *Sailor Beware*
4. 1953 Victor Mature in *The Robe*
   1954 No Award
5. 1955 Kirk Douglas in *Ulysses* and in *Indian Fighter*
6. 1956 Gregory Peck in *Moby Dick*
7. 1957 Rock Hudson in *A Farewell to Arms*
8. 1958 Kirk Douglas in *The Vikings*
9. 1959 Sal Mineo in *Tonka*

The Harvard Lampoon

THE 5 WORST ACTRESSES OF THE 1940'S

1. 1941 Betty Grable in *Wake up Screaming*
2. 1945 June Allyson in *Her Highness and the Bellboy*
3. 1946 Alexis Smith in *Night and Day*
4. 1948 Lana Turner in *The Three Musketeers*
5. 1949 Shirley Temple in *Mr. Belvedere Goes to College*

The Harvard Lampoon

Marilyn Monroe—Harvard Lampoon's *choice as the worst actress of 1952.*

THE 4 WORST ACTORS OF THE 1940'S

1. 1945 Van Johnson in *Thrill of a Romance*
2. 1946 Orson Welles in *The Stranger*
3. 1948 Burt Lancaster in *I Walk Alone*
4. 1949 Gregory Peck in *The Great Sinner*

The Harvard Lampoon

THE WORST HOLLYWOOD MUSICAL

Diva Geraldine Farrar of New York's Metropolitan Opera Company filmed a silent movie version of *Carmen* in 1915.

Bruce Felton and Mark Fowler *The Best, Worst, and Most Unusual*

Henry Fonda is one of Hollywood's most prolific stars. So far he has appeared in eighty-one movies.

15
NUMBERS

10 INTERESTING FEES PAID TO MOVIE STARS

1. In his heyday in the mid-seventies Charles Bronson made $30,000 a day, plus $2,500 a day for expenses.

2. In 1913 Fatty Arbuckle's salary for his role as a Keystone Cop was three dollars a day. Soon after, he was making $7,000 a week.

3. In 1935 Mae West was the highest paid woman in the United States. Her earnings that year were $480,833.

4. Dustin Hoffman made only $17,000 for his brilliant work in *The Graduate* in 1967; two years later he was paid $425,000 for starring in the lacklustre *John and Mary*.

5. In 1923 Clara Bow started off at $50 a week, plus her fare to Hollywood. The "It" girl went on to become one of the biggest stars of the twenties.

6. Marlon Brando has so far made $1,600,000 from his 1972 hit, *The Godfather*. He was paid $250,000 plus a share of the profits.

7. Claudette Colbert's 1942 salary of $360,000 was probably the highest in the United States that year.

8. At the height of her popularity in the twenties Mary Pickford was paid $250,000 per movie. Surprisingly, her mother was also on the payroll, receiving a flat $50,000 for each of Mary's pictures.

9. Although Bette Davis was paid only $25,000 for *What Ever Happened to Baby Jane* in 1962, she is said to have made well over a million as her percentage of the profits.

10. Rudolph Valentino received only $5 a day while making *Alimony* in 1918—and it was not even his first picture. It was his third.

HOLLYWOOD'S 10 MOST PROLIFIC STARS

1. Lon Chaney Jr.—159 movies
2. John Wayne—154
3. Myrna Loy—117
4. Mickey Rooney—116
5. Buster Crabbe—99
6. Robert Mitchum—91
7. Gary Cooper—91
8. Bette Davis—84
9. Barbara Stanwyck—84
10. Henry Fonda—81

IT HAPPENED—A LIST OF 8

1. *It Happened One Night* (1934)
2. *It Happened Tomorrow* (1944)
3. *It Happened One Summer* (1945)
4. *It Happened on 5th Avenue* (1947)
5. *It Happened in Brooklyn* (1947)
6. *It Happened to Jane* (1959)
7. *It Happened at the World's Fair* (1963)
8. *It Happened One Christmas* (1977)

THE 10 YEARS WHEN THE MOST NUMBER OF IMPORTED FILMS WERE RELEASED IN NORTH AMERICA

1. 1964—361 films
2. 1961—331
3. 1938—314
4. 1965—299
5. 1963—299

6. 1966—295
7. 1967—284
8. 1962—280
9. 1939—278
10. 1968—274

Film Daily Yearbook

THE 10 YEARS WHEN THE MOST NUMBER OF U.S. FILMS WERE RELEASED IN NORTH AMERICA

1. 1921—854 films
2. 1918—841
3. 1920—796
4. 1922—748
5. 1926—740

6. 1917—687
7. 1919—646
8. 1928—641
9. 1924—579
10. 1923—576

Film Daily Yearbook

10 FILMS WITH "ONE" IN THE TITLE

1. *It Happened One Night* (1934)
2. *One Night of Love* (1934)
3. *One Night in Lisbon* (1941)
4. *One Foot in Heaven* (1941)
5. *One Touch of Venus* (1948)
6. *One Night with You* (1948)
7. *One Minute to Zero* (1952)
8. *One Foot in Hell* (1960)
9. *One Flew Over the Cuckoo's Nest* (1975)
10. *One on One* (1977)

10 FILMS WITH "TWO" IN THE TITLE

1. *Two-Faced Woman* (1941)
2. *Two Sisters from Boston* (1946)
3. *Two Flags West* (1950)
4. *One, Two, Three* (1961)
5. *Two Women* (1961)
6. *Two Weeks in Another Town* (1962)
7. *Two for the See-Saw* (1962)
8. *Two for the Road* (1967)
9. *Two Mules for Sister Sara* (1970)
10. *Two-Minute Warning* (1976)

10 FILMS WITH "THREE" IN THE TITLE

1. *The Three Musketeers* (1935, 1939, 1948, 1974)
2. *Three Comrades* (1938)
3. *Three Came Home* (1950)
4. *Three Little Words* (1950)
5. *Three Coins in the Fountain* (1954)
6. *Three Faces of Eve* (1957)
7. *The Three Stooges Go Around the World in a Daze* (1963)
8. *Three on a Couch* (1966)
9. *Three Sisters* (1970)
10. *Three Days of the Condor* (1975)

10 FILMS WITH "FOUR" IN THE TITLE

1. *Four Men and a Prayer* (1938)
2. *Four Daughters* (2938)
3. *The Four Feathers* (1939, 1977)
4. *The 400 Blows* (1959)
5. *Four Horsemen of the Apocalypse* (1962)
6. *Four for Texas* (1963)
7. *Four Clowns* (1970)
8. *Four Flies on Grey Velvet* (1972)
9. *The Four Musketeers* (1975)
10. *The Four Deuces* (1975)

10 FILMS WITH "FIVE" IN THE TITLE

1. *Five Came Back* (1939)
2. *Five Fingers* (1952)
3. *Five Against the House* (1955)
4. *The Five Pennies* (1959)
5. *Five Branded Women* (1960)
6. *Five Weeks in a Balloon* (1962)
7. *Five Finger Exercise* (1962)
8. *Five Card Stud* (1968)
9. *Five Easy Pieces* (1970)
10. *Five Desperate Women* (1971)

5 MOVIE ACTORS WHO HAVE PLAYED ABRAHAM LINCOLN

1. Joseph Henaberry in *Birth of a Nation* (1914)
2. George A. Billings in *Abraham Lincoln* (1925)
3. Walter Huston in *Abraham Lincoln* (1930)
4. Henry Fonda in *Young Mr. Lincoln* (1939)
5. Raymond Massey in *Abe Lincoln in Illinois* (1939)

16
FIRSTS AND LASTS

THE FIRST 10 ACADEMY AWARD WINNERS
(WOMEN)

1. Janet Gaynor in *Seventh Heaven* (1927)
2. Mary Pickford in *Coquette* (1928)
3. Norma Shearer in *The Divorcée* (1929)
4. Marie Dressler in *Min and Bill* (1930)
5. Helen Hayes in *The Sin of Madelon Claudet* (1931)
6. Katharine Hepburn in *Morning Glory* (1932)
7. Claudette Colbert in *It Happened One Night* (1934)
8. Bette Davis in *Dangerous* (1935)
9. Luise Rainer in *The Great Ziegfeld* (1936)
10. Luise Rainer in *The Good Earth* (1937)

THE FIRST 10 ACADEMY AWARD WINNERS (MEN)

1. Emil Jannings in *The Way of All Flesh* (1927)
2. Warner Baxter in *Old Arizona* (1928)
3. George Arliss in *Disraeli* (1929)
4. Lionel Barrymore in *A Free Soul* (1930)
5. Fredric March in *Dr. Jekyll and Mr. Hyde* (1931)
6. Wallace Beery in *The Champ* (1931)
7. Charles Laughton in *The Private Life of Henry VIII* (1932)
8. Clark Gable in *It Happened One Night* (1934)
9. Victor McLaglen in *The Informer* (1935)
10. Paul Muni in *The Story of Louis Pasteur* (1936)

10 MOVIES IN WHICH FAMOUS STARS MADE THEIR FEATURE FILM DEBUT

1. Humphrey Bogart in *A Devil with Women* (1930)
2. Clark Gable in *The Painted Desert* (1931)
3. Bette Davis in *Bad Sister* (1931)
4. Shirley Temple in *Red-Haired Alibi* (1932)
5. Cary Grant in *This Is the Night* (1932)
6. Mae West in *Night after Night* (1932)
7. William Holden in *Golden Boy* (1939)
8. Sidney Greenstreet in *The Maltese Falcon* (1941)
9. Elizabeth Taylor in *Lassie Come Home* (1943)
10. Jane Fonda in *Tall Story* (1960)

10 MORE FAMOUS MOVIE DEBUTS

1. Marlon Brando in *The Men* (1950)
2. Clint Eastwood in *Revenge of the Creature* (1955)
3. Steve McQueen in *Never Love a Stranger* (1958)
4. Warren Beatty in *Splendor in the Grass* (1961)
5. Julie Andrews in *Mary Poppins* (1964)
6. Raquel Welch in *Roustabout* (1964)
7. Woody Allen in *What's New, Pussycat?* (1965)
8. Richard Dreyfuss in *The Graduate* (1967)
9. Robert DeNiro in *Greetings* (1968)
10. Diane Keaton in *Lovers and Other Strangers* (1970)

10 FAMOUS MOVIE "FIRSTS"

1. *First Comes Courage* (1943)
   with Merle Oberon and Brian Aherne
2. *First Yank Into Tokyo* (1945)
   with Barbara Hale
3. *The First Legion* (1951)
   with Charles Boyer and Barbara Rush
4. *The First Travelling Saleslady* (1956)
   with Clint Eastwood, Ginger Rogers, and Carol Channing
5. *The First Texan* (1956)
   with Joel McCrea

6. *First Man into Space* (1959)
     with Marshall Thompson
7. *First Spaceship on Venus* (1960)
     with Yoko Tani
8. *First to Fight* (1967)
     with Dean Jagger and Gene Hackman
9. *The First Time* (1969)
     with Jacqueline Bissett
10. *First Love* (1970)
     with Maximilian Schell and Dominique Sanda

10 FAMOUS MOVIE "LASTS"

1. *The Last Days of Pompeii* (1935)
     with Basil Rathbone and Louis Calhern
2. *The Last Time I Saw Paris* (1954)
     with Elizabeth Taylor and Van Johnson
3. *The Last 10 Days* (1956)
     with Oskar Werner and Lotte Tobisch
4. *Last Summer* (1969)
     with Richard Thomas and Barbara Hershey
5. *The Last Picture Show* (1971)
     with Ellen Burstyn and Cloris Leachman
6. *The Last of the Red Hot Lovers* (1972)
     with Allan Arkin and Sally Kellerman
7. *The Last Detail* (1973)
     with Jack Nicholson
8. *Last Tango in Paris* (1973)
     with Marlon Brando and Maria Schneider
9. *The Last Tycoon* (1976)
     with Robert DeNiro and Jack Nicholson
10. *The Last Remake of Beau Geste* (1977)
     with Marty Feldman and Ann Margaret

Judy Garland, one of America's best-loved stars, made her final appearance in 1963. Above, as she looked in 1943, at the height of her career.

Spencer Tracy made 74 movies, the last of which was Guess Who's Coming to Dinner? *(1967). In* The Old Man and the Sea *(above), made in 1958, he gave one of his best performances.*

10 FINAL APPEARANCES

1. Jean Harlow in *Saratoga* (1937)
2. Humphrey Bogart in *The Harder They Fall* (1956)
3. Errol Flynn in *Cuban Rebel Girls* (1959)
4. Gary Cooper in *The Naked Edge* (1961)
5. Charles Laughton in *Advise and Consent* (1962)
6. Judy Garland in *I Could Go on Singing* (1963)
7. Vivien Leigh in *Ship of Fools* (1965)
8. Montgomery Clift in *The Defector* (1966)
9. Spencer Tracy in *Guess Who's Coming to Dinner?* (1967)
10. John Wayne in *The Shootist* (1976)